The Scarsdale Nutritionist's Weight Loss Cookbook

JUDITH R. CORLIN, Ed.M., R.D.
and
MARY SUSAN MILLER

A Fireside Book
Published by Simon and Schuster
NEW YORK

A Fireside Book
Published by Simon and Schuster
A Division of Gulf & Western Corporation
Simon & Schuster Building
Rockefeller Center
1230 Avenue of the Americas
New York, New York 10020
FIRESIDE and colophon are registered trademarks of Simon & Schuster.
Designed by Stanley S. Drate
Manufactured in the United States of America
Printed and bound by Fairfield Graphics
1 • 3 • 5 • 7 • 9 • 10 • 8 • 6 • 4 • 2
Library of Congress Cataloging in Publication Data

Corlin, Judith R.
The Scarsdale nutritionist's weight loss cookbook.

"A Fireside book."
Includes index.
1. Reducing diets—Recipes. I. Miller, Mary Susan.
II. Title.
RM222.2.C644   1982   641.5′635   82-10758
ISBN: 0-671-45794-2

To a world of diet-discouraged people
—here is the LITE WAY of life.

Contents

Introduction

Americans have seen the light! In the florescent glare of super-markets shoppers are dazzled by an array of new foods labeled "light" or with a slimmer spelling, "lite." They tempt appetites with goodies ranging from beer, 150 calories for regular down to a mere 100 for light, to once-forbidden fruits, which in the lite can have over one third fewer calories.

Meanwhile, we continually reach for books and articles warning us about food-related diseases such as hypertension and heart trouble. Eat right and stay healthy, they say. As food, therefore, builds a pathway to health as well as to slim good looks, the lure of lite foods grows.

And why not? Lite food offers assurances of our right to life, by keeping us well; to liberty, by letting us eat the foods we love; and to happiness, by making true the American dream of Thin. Yet questions arise.

• *Are commercial lite foods really better for your health?*

Generally, they eliminate calories that regular commercial foods have in abundance. How many calories they eliminate differs with each product, for the Food and Drug Administration has not yet caught up to the lite food binge by requiring a legal definition of lite. The FDA has determined that "reduced calorie" foods must have a third fewer calories than comparable regular products and that "low calorie" foods may have no more than forty calories per portion. Lite foods, however, still remain on their own.

Lite foods may aid health too by reducing certain other food groups, such as fat.

• *Do lite foods really help you lose weight?*

The fewer calories you take in, the fewer pounds you add. Those commercial lite foods that have fewer calories aid in weight reduction and weight maintenance.

9

• *Do lite foods taste good?*

For the most part lite foods taste as good as their more caloric counterparts. Their real value, however, lies in the fact that they enable you to eat your favorite foods at the cost of fewer calories. In that way you are less likely to become a yo-yo dieter, depriving yourself of everything "good" until you can no longer stand it, and then breaking loose on a guilt-producing food binge. With lite foods, even the strictest dieters can eat spaghetti sauce, pancakes, hot chocolate, and between-meal snacks. That way, they are not emotionally deprived while either losing pounds or maintaining the weight they want.

Though helpful in several ways, commercial lite foods are not *The Answer* for which the eating world has been waiting. They have serious drawbacks:

Their variety is limited. While you may stay on a diet of lite canned fruit and frozen dinners longer than you would stick to cottage cheese and Rye Krisps, you will invariably grow bored. There is simply not enough variety in lite foods to withstand the call of a Big Mac with french fries or of veal parmesan with spaghetti. You need more leeway.

• *Many lite foods fail to fulfill the promise that the fashionably-slim people offer in advertisements. For one thing, lite foods often sound lighter than they are: does it really help to save 7 calories in a glop of catsup? While lite maple syrup may save a third of the calorie count and lite salad dressing a half, both add too many calories you do not need. Similarly, why eat lite ice cream when alternative desserts which are just as delicious and far more calorie-saving can be prepared at home?*

• *Lite foods are expensive. A national lite syrup increased its sales by 50% in the summer of 1980 alone, not only by pouring more syrup on America's pancakes, but by making consumers pay more for the bottles from which they poured. Why lite foods cost more than their regular counterparts on supermarket shelves no one says for sure, but their popularity seems to be a logical guess: good old supply and demand. While the manufacturer probably spends less to produce them, you have to pay about 20% more for lite canned fruits, upwards of 12% more for lite mayonnaise, and as much as 100% more for frozen lite dinners.*

It appears, therefore, that although lite foods make eating more healthful and dieting less painful, commercial lite products fall short of expectations.

So what are you to do? Must you choose between starvation and a future of lettuce leaves and seltzer water or abandonment to calorie-laden food, bad health, and overweight? No. There is a third course: You can prepare your own lite meals, and as a result,

- *have limitless variety;*
- *save hundreds of calories;*
- *eat healthfully;*
- *cook and eat your favorite foods;*
- *give your budget a break.*

With a little help you can become an expert lite foods chef, and be so creative that your menus will dazzle. The Scarsdale Nutritionist's Weight Loss Cookbook provides that help. Here you will find recipes for each course in your meal, delicious enough to please the palate of the most demanding gourmet and so low in calories only the cook will believe it.

What Is the Lite Way to Eat?

- The Lite Way eliminates some calorie dense foods.
- The Lite Way uses foods that are high in bulk and water.
- The Lite Way portion-controls other calorie dense foods.
- The Lite Way reduces salt.

CALORIE-DENSE FOODS

Fat, sugar, and starch have the highest concentration of calories. They are, in other words, "calorie dense."

Fat.

In America's typical diet, about 40% of the calories come from fat, the largest contributor of calories. If that sounds too much like a nutritionist speaking, try this: it may take over 100 ears of corn to make two-thirds of a cup of oil—the amount you use to make salad dressing; it takes only about 20 kernels of corn—less than a row in a single ear—to pop the same two-thirds of a cup of popcorn. The oil has over 1300 calories; the popcorn has about

16. That's the difference between calorie dense and non-calorie dense foods.

The *Scarsdale Nutritionist's Weight Loss Cookbook* gives you recipes with alternatives to the high fat cheeses, beef, and cream that you used to consider essential to a company meal. It gives you preparation hints and provides low fat substitutes that add taste and variety to your meals, not pounds. You will:

- broil meat to brown it instead of braising it in oil;
- use plain lowfat yogurt in place of sour cream;
- poach instead of frying, or fry the Lite Way;
- pass up meat marbleized with fat for leaner cuts;
- avoid high fat fish (p. 99);
- tenderize fat-low meats by marinating;
- make your own low-calorie salad dressings, even mayonnaise;
- find new ways to prepare lean chicken, turkey, and fish;
- broil with wine instead of butter (85% of the calories in the wine burn off);
- stir fry instead of deep fry;
- turn dry skim milk into a look-alike for cream;
- chill soups and stews to lift off the fat;
- discover the wonders of buttermilk;
- let low fat cottage cheese play taste tricks for you;
- top dishes with grated Parmesan cheese instead of cheddar;
- adventure into new tastes with herbs;
- and do dozens of other things.

Sugar.

Sugar is the second calorie dense culprit. Take an orange: it contains only 39 calories while an 8 ounce glass of orange juice contains 112. Similarly, a peeled apple (1 cup, chopped) has 53 calories; enough dried apples to make a cup has 150 calories. The latter is calorie dense.

The Lite Way cuts down on sugar and teaches you to:

- use gelatin instead of sweetened Jello in dessert recipes (0% sugar as opposed to 85% sugar);
- top desserts with fruit and Lite Way "whipped cream" instead of syrups;
- whip up sugarless summer drinks that are sweet, and sinfully tasty;
- be alert for hidden sugar in commercial products such as cereals, condiments, and crackers;
- identify so-called "health" foods high in sugar, like granola and wheat germ;

- dress up fruits to replace cake and cookies;
- prepare sundaes and frappes the Lite Way;
- satisfy your sweet tooth with a touch of jelly, Lite Way cheese-cake, and chocolate mousse;
- and more and more and more.

GOOD NEWS: A new low calorie sweetener called Aspartame will soon appear on the market with an all-clear from the Food and Drug Administration. It is 180 times sweeter than table sugar and has 0.1 calories per teaspoon. Aspartame does not have the bitter aftertaste of saccharine or its possible risk as a carcinogen. While not effective in cooking or baking, since it loses its sweetness under prolonged heat, Aspartame's main role will be as a table sugar substitute and sugar replacement in dry food products such as coffee and tea, drink mixes, dairy products, puddings, gelatins, and toppings. For example, lemonade may be reduced in calories from 86 to 5 and chocolate pudding made with skim milk may be reduced from 150 to 75 calories.

Starch

Starchy food can be calorie dense. While ½ cup of a starchy vegetable like lima beans, for instance, contains up to 94 calories, the same portion of non-starchy green beans totals only 17. A slice of bread averages about 75 calories, but a mere ½ cup of bread crumbs, far more dense, contains 228 calories.

The Lite Way cuts down on starchy foods. You will:

- eliminate floury gravies and sauces (and never miss them!);
- thicken with corn starch instead of flour (same number of calories, but less is needed);
- make stuffing with vegetables instead of breads, or with less bread;
- purée vegetables to use as sauces;
- make your own low-calorie muffins;
- use bean sprouts along with rice in casseroles;
- cut down on the breading in veal parmesan;
- discover new vegetables and a world of low-starch menus;
- think more about the *fat* you put on your starch, since it has twice the calories than equal amounts of starch.

Bulk and Water Foods

Calories do not measure quantity. Your stomach does not cry out "Enough!" after its calorie quota for a meal. On the contrary, it may keep asking for more. What fills you is bulk—the fiber and water content of foods.

High Bulk	*Low Bulk*
1 cup bran cereal with skim milk	2 large pancakes
2 slices of rye toast without butter	maple syrup (4 tablespoons)
1 orange	1 glass of orange juice
1 poached egg	coffee with sugar and cream
black coffee	
TOTAL CALORIES: 450	TOTAL CALORIES: 650

The high bulk breakfast has given your stomach more bulk to satisfy its hunger, while the low bulk breakfast has given it only more calories. Since stomachs do not count calories, yours probably will be asking for something more to eat a short while after the pancakes have been washed down with maple syrup, orange juice, and sugared coffee with cream. The bulk of bran, rye toast, and an orange should hold you until lunch.

Sometimes when you think you are hungry, your emotions rather than your stomach are calling for food. You may be under stress or bored; you may have just finished a piece of work and need to reward yourself. You want to eat. It is not so much swallowing food as chewing it that brings satisfaction at those times. And what offers better chewing but bulk.

High Bulk	*Calories*	*Low Bulk*	*Calories*
1 cup fresh mushrooms	65	1 cup cream of mushroom soup	140
large tangerine	44	medium banana	100
medium apple	80	1/2 cup applesauce	105
TOTAL CALORIES	189	TOTAL CALORIES	345

By selecting high bulk in place of low bulk foods, it is obvious that you can fill your stomach as well as your need to chew, and do it with a minimum of calories.

Smaller Portions (Portion Control)

Most of us have been raised on the belief that we must eat everything on our plate, or else; the "or else" ranging from loss of dessert to guilt over starving children somewhere in the world. Since most of us are also raised on the notion that bigger is better, food tempts us by its enormity: Big Macs, double-dip cones, and 16-ounce steaks dripping over the sides of the plate, as well as luring advertisements to "Eat all you can."

Even at home, the portions we serve are far larger than our appetites or nutritional requirements. Yet there it is on the plate and what do we do? Eat it, or else. Unfortunately, the outcome is not less hunger around the world, but more overweight and health problems right here in America.

The Lite Way guides you in preparing sensible portions of those good foods you love, but know are calorie dense. You may be surprised at the calories you save when you learn the knack of portion control during meals or while snacking. For example:

3 ounce sirloin steak . . . . 320 calories
12 ounce sirloin steak . . . . .1280 calories
                    SAVING: 960 calories

4 dates . . . . 76 calories
1 cup dates. . . . . 470 calories
                    SAVING: 394 calories

1 ounce granola . . . . 70 calories
1 cup granola . . . . 560 calories
                    SAVING: 490 calories

2 tablespoons peanut butter. . . . . .190 calories
½ cup peanut butter . . . . .800 calories
                    SAVINGS: 610 calories

Salt

While small amounts of salt in our food intake are essential for good health, large amounts may contribute to hypertension. For this reason millions of Americans have learned the art of low salt cooking on direct orders from their physicians. Millions of others have learned from their scales: for them salt contributes to water retention in body tissues.

The payoff for both of these groups of salt-avoiders has been better health, better looks, and one thing more: the discovery of new food tastes. Where they had previously disguised foods under a blanket of salt, they now are able to savor each dish for its own unique taste. Since fruits, vegetables, dairy products, fish, and poultry reach us with enough of their own natural salt to keep our bodies healthy and to taste delicious, the Lite Way offers recipes in which very little salt has been added. You will find that good food does not need to have the same salty taste, and that it can have a spectrum of flavors that you never knew existed.

- What does a potato taste like?
- What is the flavor of a tomato?
- How about the taste of rice?
- Does chicken have a taste?
- What is the taste of a string bean?

Recipes in this book will lead you to the answers and teach you millions of ways to create flavors without salt.

Why Not Calories?

You will find no calorie figures for the recipes in this cookbook. You do not need them. Through the *Weight Loss Cookbook* you can become a creative cook, not a food analyst. You will change your eating style and your tastes. You do not have to watch calories since the recipes do that for you. You need not guess about calories, wonder, or experiment. You will know and recognize what tastes good and what is low in calories. In the front of each food section, important calorie comparisons have been made which you will need in order to understand how to prepare everything the Lite Way, from soups to desserts, with snacks in between. Instead of having to think calories and diet, you will think style and experience tastes. And you will truly *understand* the Lite Way of life.

Calories are tricksters. They can fool you in more than one way, and undoubtedly have in the past.

- Have you noticed how no two calorie charts list the same count? An ounce of Gouda cheese may vary in calories from 85 to 115, depending on the chart you consult. Even the most conscientious cook is bound to blunder; that's why the *Weight Loss Cookbook* says, "Let the Lite Way recipes teach you the big principles that apply to all calorie-lite foods."
- No one can control factors that affect the calorie count of foods. *It is an inexact measurement.* For instance, wheats from

different soils have different calorie counts. Therefore, a slice of bread baked from those separate wheats will differ, and so will the meat from the cattle that ate that wheat. Isn't it little wonder that calorie charts are confusing?

What's the Difference?

The Lite Way provides more than recipes for meal time; it provides recipes for a lifetime. It gives more than a new style of eating; it gives a new style of living. It beckons you to wake up to a new day, in which you are in control of your body. All of America is seeing the potential for a long life, a healthy life, a life of strength and good looks; and that potential is food. The Lite Way is the right way.

America's leading gourmet chefs have joined the move to lite eating, making "lite" the rich sauces, buttery desserts and oil marinades for which they were famous. They agree that health comes first, as they create alternatives. With *The Scarsdale Nutritionist's Weight Loss Cookbook* you can create with them. Like James Beard you will "sauté" in homemade stock instead of butter, and like Julia Child you will "fry" eggs in a covered nonstick pan with a little water. Like the chef at Brooklyn's elegant River Café you will turn your beef dishes into chicken recipes, and like La Caravelle's André Moisan, you will no longer fry fish but broil it without oil or fry the Lite Way.

You will become an international cook. Your Italian dishes will have more tomatoes and herbs and less oil. Your Chinese dishes will be stir-fried in a wok with less oil. Your sandwiches will be Danish, with one slice of bread. Your French cuisine will be *minceur,* or low calorie. You will be Middle Eastern with your use of yogurt and tropical with your use of fruit. With spices your meals will travel the world over.

What you will do with plain old American cooking will make you think you have discovered a new country. You will bake potatoes longer in order to make the skin extra crisp; that way they taste good without butter. You will marinate chicken at room temperature in lemon juice for an hour or longer to bring out new flavor. You will stuff a turkey with chopped onion, cabbage, and celery made zesty with caraway seeds and wonder why you used to limit yourself to bread stuffing. You will top salads with bean sprouts instead of croutons, grate Parmesan on cauliflower, sprinkle vinegar on brussels sprouts, make sandwiches on half a hollowed out bagel, and create egg dishes with extra egg whites to reduce calories and cholesterol.

Does it make a difference? Let's compare a few meals and recipes the Lite Way with the way you used to make them.

If you eat the Lite Way	*Instead of . . .*	*You'll save calories*
	In The Morning	
tomato juice (1 cup)	grape juice (1 cup)	110
1 poached egg	1 fried egg	50
Puffed Wheat (1 cup)	Grape Nuts (1 cup)	365
1 teaspoon diet margarine	1 teaspoon butter	160
1 ounce Canadian bacon	1 ounce bacon	55
skim milk	chocolate milk	120
	At Lunch	
tuna in water (3½ ounce)	tuna in oil (3½ ounce)	70
Lite Way mayonnaise (1 tablespoon)	regular mayonnaise (1 tablespoon)	65
Lite Way milk shake	regular thick shake	240
lumpy apple sauce and yogurt flavored with cinnamon	slice of apple pie	200
	At Dinner	
Lite Way veal parmesan	regular veal parmesan	585
baked potato (2½ inches long)	fried potatoes (1 cup)	380
Lite Way candied squash	regular candied squash	210
salad with Lite Way dressing	salad with oil-based dressing	140
Lite Way lemon pie	lemon meringue pie	235

That difference would save you . . .

  860 calories at breakfast
  575 calories at lunch
1550 calories at dinner
_____
2985 calories for 1 day

VEAL with MUSHROOMS

The Old Way	Calories	The Lite Way	Calories
2 veal chops (loin without tail)	528	3 ounces veal scallops (braised, drained)	200
2 tablespoons butter	200	1 tablespoon bread crumbs	25
4 large mushrooms	32	1 tablespoon grated Parmesan cheese	21
1 small onion	30	Freshly grated nutmeg	
1 small tomato	25	Onion powder	
½ cup stock	25	Pepper	
1 clove garlic		Salt	
Salt		½ cup mushrooms	28
Pepper		2 tablespoons sherry wine	40
Thyme			314
¼ cup bread crumbs	100		
	940		

VEAL PARMESAN

The Old Way	Calories	The Lite Way	Calories
3 ounces veal	200	3 ounces veal	200
3 tablespoons fat	330	1 tablespoon grated Parmesan	21
¼ cup bread crumbs	100	1 tablespoon bread crumbs	25
2 tablespoons flour	25	1 tablespoon part-skim mozzarella	50
½ cup meat sauce	125	¾ cup tomato juice	35
2 tablespoons grated Parmesan cheese	42		331
2 tablespoons mozzarella	95		
	917		

Martyrs never lose weight. They merely deprive themselves of "good" food, agonize as long as they can stand it, then forget the diet and go on a binge. Martyrdom diets do not work for them, and they won't work for you. *The Scarsdale Nutritionist's Weight Loss Cookbook* lets you treat yourself well:

• You won't have to sit down to a bare plate of cottage cheese. The Lite Way makes food pretty as well as healthful.
• You won't have to give up between meal snacks. The Lite Way gives you recipes for nibbling, like popcorn with butter flavoring or your own homemade "garp."

- You won't have to bid farewell to the gooey desserts you dream of. The Lite Way allows you to create look-alikes that taste so good you will almost think you are cheating.
- You won't know any longer which foods are "good" and which are "good for you." *The Weight Loss Cookbook* will turn your preconceived notions upside down.

What is the miracle? No miracle; just recipes for making old foods new ways.

The Scarsdale Nutritionist's Weight Loss Cookbook holds out no false promises—like a 10-pound weight loss per week or "Eat all the apple pie you want and lose a pound a day." It gives you instead the true promise of a new eating style that will alter your taste forever. You will discover the creative cook you never expected to be and delight your friends and family with elegant gourmet dishes that are good for you. Once you try the Lite Way, you will never return to the old way of cooking. And you will never have to "diet" again for the Lite Way keeps you the way you want to be.

If you don't believe it, see what you have left behind:

Food	Pounds gained in a year
1 teaspoon butter to fry an egg	4.7
1 teaspoon sugar in tea	2.1
1 teaspoon vegetable oil to broil	10.4
1 cup whole milk with lunch	7.4
1 tablespoon mayonnaise in salad	10.4
1 tablespoon French dressing on lettuce	6.25
3 soda crackers crumbled in bouillon	5.2
1 large cookie for dessert	10.4
10 potato chips for a snack	7.4

If you ate just those items every day for a year above your calorie needs the weight gain would total an extra 64 pounds! While that seems a near impossibility and there may be individual differences in the way your body uses food that can alter this count, a clear fact emerges: the old way of cooking leads to overweight. Whether by 10 pounds or 64, overweight is destructive to your health, your looks, and your self-image.

The Scarsdale Nutritionist's Weight Loss Cookbook lets you be a new person in the new world of food.

General Rules for Cooking the Lite Way

1. Cut down the amount of oil in regular recipes. Use nonstick pans, and/or a vegetable cooking spray for lite "frying."
2. 'Use chicken, turkey, fish, veal, seafood, and only lean beef.
3. Remove all visible fat from chicken, turkey, fish, and beef before cooking, during (broil on a rack), or after cooking.
4. Buy lean and young. For example, ½ pound of regular ground beef is 800 calories as opposed to 300 calories for ½ pound of lean ground beef. A 1-pound young broiler is 273 calories; a 1-pound hen is 708 calories.
5. Experiment with Lite Way flavorings of wine and herbs; and cut back on salt.
6. Emphasize fresh foods, limiting heavy sugar syrups, fatty and floury gravies, and highly salted processed foods.
7. Prepare homemade chicken, beef, or vegetable stock. Or use "½ and ½" regular bouillon mixed with salt free bouillon to reduce salt.
8. Make "cream" soup using pureed vegetables, buttermilk, yogurt, dry skim or evaporated skim milk as thickeners, instead of butter, cream, or flour.
9. Prepare high-bulk nibblers, which are low in calories, fat, and sugar.
10. Prepare desserts which look and taste "illegal" but are made with limited sugar, limited fat, and limited artificial sweeteners.
11. Use lowfat cheeses in food preparation.
12. Use limited amounts of fat, flour, sugar, and salt in salad dressings, sauces, and gravies.
13. Use imitation mayonnaise or make your own Lite Way mayonnaise. Or add 1 tablespoon mayonnaise to one cup lowfat yogurt.
14. Use bouillon or Lite Way stock instead of oil when a recipe calls for braising. Each tablespoon of fat you omit saves you 150 calories.
15. Sauté the Lite Way: cook garlic, onion (and/or vegetables preferred, such as shallots, mushrooms, or peppers, in ½-¾ cup bouillon or stock until vegetables are tender. Add fish or poultry and cook as if "sautéing." Or, you may add your choice of broth, tomato juice, or wine and bake or stew. Lowfat yogurt or butter-

milk may be added near end of cooking time for a lowfat enrichment.

16. Use the natural sweetening ability of fruits and fruit juices for desserts, while limiting sugar, honey, and molasses. Use only small amounts of artificial sweeteners.

17. Use lowfat cottage cheese, lowfat yogurt, buttermilk, tomato juice, or bouillon as a base for salad dressings, instead of high-fat cheeses, sour cream, cream cheese, and oil.

18. For marinating and basting when broiling or grilling, replace oil or fat with fresh lemon or lime juice; vinegar; vegetable, beef or chicken broth or bouillon; tomato juice; non-fat milk products; or wine.

19. Potato, rice, and noodles need not be eliminated as too starchy, but rather their creamy, high-fat dressings should be eliminated. Try fresh and dried herbs, chives, scallions, imitation bacon bits, grated Parmesan and lowfat cheeses, fresh pepper or lowfat yogurt as toppings.

20. Prepare a library of homemade vinegars by adding herbs such as tarragon, chives, rosemary, and sage to cider or wine vinegar. Use these vinegars often instead of butter, high-fat cheeses, and cream sauces.

21. Extend chopped beef with grated vegetables from which excess moisture has been squeezed.

22. Use fresh garlic or onion, or garlic or onion powder, instead of garlic or onion salt.

Herbs, Spices, Wines and Garnish

For the Lite Way gourmet, try:

- sherry and watercress in chicken soup;
- bean sprouts and/or mushrooms in chicken soup;
- raw vegetable bits in cold soups;
- buttermilk or plain lowfat yogurt instead of cream in cold vegetable soups;
- plain lowfat yogurt and cinnamon or a tablespoon of vanilla or coffee or lemon yogurt to garnish fresh or stewed fruit;
- capers, chopped anchovies, or poppyseeds in salads;
- crushed garlic in vinegar for salads;
- Dijon-style mustard or curry powder in salad dressing;
- sesame seeds, scallions, or chives in salad dressing;
- buttermilk or plain lowfat yogurt to thicken dressings or sauces;

- basil in raw or cooked tomato paste or purée;
- anise or fennel seeds in fish dishes;
- caraway ("rye" taste) for dips;
- cayenne for red hot dip or marinade;
- chives for onion in omelets or dips;
- dill in sauce for fresh salmon;
- a bit of ginger in a stir-fry or marinades;
- mint for tea, lamb, and sauces;
- Dijon-style mustard for marinades and sauces;
- oregano for "Southern Italy" tomato sauce;
- sweet tarragon and fennel to vegetables;
- butter-flavoring or other extracts such as maple, chocolate, rum, brandy, lemon, and banana to add taste without calories;
- dry table wines for cooking instead of sweet wines which add sugar calories and cooking wines which add extra salt; lite calorie beers or distilled spirits also leave few extra calories;
- fresh basil on cold sliced tomatoes;
- snipped chives as a garnish on cold soups;
- dill in cottage cheese;
- lovage (tastes and looks like celery) in poaching liquid for shrimp;
- mint in carrots, peas or green beans;
- a fresh sprig of rosemary in a roasting chicken;
- sorrel in poached chicken;
- oregano in fish soup;
- sage in Manhattan clam chowder;
- tarragon on broiled fish;
- fresh chervil or hints of anise at the last minute to your omelet;
- fennel in carrots or beets;
- crumbled marjoram into mushroom salad;
- savory with scrambled eggs;
- plain lowfat yogurt, dried mustard, and cumin seeds for cold poached chicken;
- plain lowfat yogurt, lemon, minced onion, garlic, cinnamon, curry, pepper, clove, and cumin for lamb;
- marinating chicken and lamb in lemon and/or lime juice;
- poaching fish or chicken in apple juice;
- add a pinch of chili powder for broiled tomatoes;
- add cinnamon for broiled squash;
- vinegar in a soup or stew for "salty" flavor;
- cooking vegetables crisp in broth with lemon juice or wine;
- using eggplant or zucchini as a base for pizza;
- making homemade herb blends like the three following.

ITALIAN SEASONING

MAKES ABOUT 6 TABLESPOONS.

2   teaspoons each dried basil and oregano
2   teaspoons minced, dried parsley
2   teaspoons each dried rosemary and thyme
1   teaspoon each paprika and coarsely
    ground black pepper

Just mix ingredients together and store in a tightly covered container.

SALAD HERBS

MAKES ABOUT 6 TABLESPOONS.

2½   teaspoons minced, dried parsley
2   teaspoons chopped, dried chives
1   teaspoon each dried thyme and basil
1   teaspoon each dried dill weed and tarragon

Mix all ingredients well and store in a tightly covered container.

LEMON PEPPER SEASONING

MAKES ABOUT 6 TABLESPOONS.

4   tablespoons coarsely ground black pepper
2   tablespoons grated lemon zest

Shake pepper and lemon rind in a tightly covered container and store in the refrigerator.

SOUPS

Soup was commonly considered by some as the opener to a seven course dinner, but now it is prepared as a main dish. Soup and salad or a sandwich frequently appear on lunch menus, and "Soup time" is the cry of many a mother as her children rush home from school for a quick lunch. Whether served as an appetizer or an entree, soup, both nutritious and delicious, is here to stay.

The calorie count for individual servings of commercial soups can widely vary:

Soup	Calorie Count per Cup
Bouillon	10
Chicken Noodle	110
Manhattan Clam Chowder	111
Oyster Stew	142
New England Clam Chowder	157
Bean	190

Even these counts are only estimates, since different brands have different calorie counts for the same kind of soup. For instance: vegetable soup ranges from 42 to 150 calories per cup; tomato soup from 60 to 170 calories per cup; and pea soup from 73 to 186 calories per cup.

The only way you can be sure of a low calorie count is to make your own. Our Lite Way soup recipes are all low in calories and high in taste without the high salt content of commercially prepared soups.

GENERAL SUGGESTIONS FOR LITE WAY SOUP

1. Cut the calories in cream soups by using evaporated skimmed milk, lowfat yogurt, or buttermilk instead of regular heavy cream.

25

2. Thicken soups by using puréed vegetables instead of flour.

3. Use homemade chicken stock or bouillon (10 calories per cup) instead of butter (100 calories per tablespoon) as a starter for soup.

4. For a quick soup, pour hot bouillon over water chestnuts, pea pods, bean sprouts or mushrooms, or an assortment of any of your favorite raw vegetables.

5. Instead of starchy rice or noodles, use additional vegetables such as bean sprouts, or limit the amounts of rice and noodles.

6. Use homemade soup stock as soup base, gravy base, or as flavoring for vegetable cooking.

7. For easy storage, freeze stock in ice cube trays. Then store cubes in plastic bags in the freezer and use in amounts as needed.

8. Save leftover vegetables and poultry, and poultry and meat bones to add strength to stock.

LITE WAY BEEF, VEAL, OR CHICKEN STOCK
MAKES 10 1-CUP SERVINGS.

> 4 pounds beef bones or 6 pounds veal neck and shank bones or 3 pounds chicken pieces
> 2 cups coarsley chopped onions
> 2 cups coarsley chopped carrots
> 3 or 4 celery stalks
> 2 or 3 bouillon cubes (chicken, beef, or vegetable)
> Salt and pepper to taste

Combine meaty beef bones including knuckles *or* veal shank and neck bones or chicken pieces with onions, carrots, and celery stalks in 4 qt. pot. Cover with cold water. Bring to boil and remove and discard "scum" which rises to top. Add bouillon cubes and salt and pepper to taste. Simmer 3 hours covered. Taste and reseason. Strain and chill. Skim all fat from surface or refrigerate stock over night, and lift congealed fat from top.

For thicker stock:
Strain and discard bones. Purée vegetables in batches in food processor or blender. Return to stock.

BROCCOLI SOUP

MAKES 6 SERVINGS.

> 2 cups Lite Way Chicken Stock (page 26), or 2 cups water + 3 bouillon cubes
> 2 cups chopped broccoli
> 1 cup buttermilk
> 1/2 teaspoon basil
> 1/2 teaspoon tarragon
> Salt and pepper to taste
> Small pieces raw broccoli
> Plain lowfat yogurt
> Snipped fresh chives

Combine stock and chopped broccoli in saucepan. Gently boil until broccoli is tender (10-12 minutes). Cool. Process in food processor or blender in batches until smooth. Add basil, tarragon, buttermilk, and salt and pepper. Garnish each serving with small pieces of raw broccoli, a dab of yogurt, and a sprinkling of snipped chives. Serve hot or cold.

YELLOW AND GREEN SQUASH SOUP

MAKES 4-6 SERVINGS.

> 1 small onion, chopped
> 2 1/4 cups Lite Way Chicken Stock (page 26) or bouillon
> 3 cups chopped green and/or yellow summer squash
> 1/2 cup buttermilk or 1/2 cup plain lowfat yogurt
> Small pieces of raw squash
> Snipped fresh chives

Cook onion in 1/4 cup stock in saucepan until tender. Add chopped squash and 2 cups stock. Gently boil until squash is soft. Cool. Blend in food processor or blender in batches only until thick. Add buttermilk or yogurt. Garnish with bits of squash and chives.

LITE SPINACH SOUP
MAKES 4 SERVINGS.

  1 pound chopped spinach
  3 cups Lite Way Chicken Stock (page 26)
  1 teaspoon fresh lemon juice
     Salt and pepper to taste
 1/2 cup buttermilk or 1/4 cup skim milk solids
     Lite Way Sour Cream #1 (page 172)
     Diced cucumbers

Cook spinach in chicken stock in saucepan just until spinach is limp (2-3 min.). Cool. Add lemon juice, and salt and pepper. Add buttermilk or dry skim milk. Garnish with Lite Way sour cream and diced cucumbers.

COOL CUCUMBER SOUP
MAKES 3-4 SERVINGS.

  2 cups chopped cucumber
 1/2 cup chopped onion
  1 teaspoon chopped fresh dill
  1 cup buttermilk
     Fresh parsley
     Snipped fresh chives or green onion

Blend cucumber, onion, and dill in batches in food processor or blender. Blend in buttermilk. Chill. Garnish with parsley, and chives or green onion.

ONION SOUP
MAKES 3-4 SERVINGS.

  3 large onions, chopped
 3 1/2 cups Lite Way Chicken Stock (page 26) or 1/2-1/2 bouillon
     Salt and pepper to taste
  1 teaspoon soy sauce
     Grated Parmesan cheese

Cook onion in 1/4 cup Lite Way Chicken Stock in saucepan until tender (8-10 min.). Add 3 cups chicken stock; cook until heated through. Season with salt and pepper. Add soy sauce. Sprinkle with Parmesan cheese.

FROTHY VEGETABLE SOUP
MAKES 2-3 SERVINGS.

2   cups Lite Way Chicken Stock (page 26)
1   zucchini, sliced
2   carrots, sliced
1   celery stalk, sliced
    Dash nutmeg
    Salt and pepper to taste.

Combine all ingredients in medium saucepan. Bring to boil; reduce heat and simmer covered 15 to 20 minutes or until the vegetables are tender. Purée in batches in a blender for 30 seconds. Serve hot in mugs.

CHILLED TOMATO SOUP
MAKES 2-3 SERVINGS.

3   cups pureed fresh tomatoes
2   tablespoons tomato paste
4   scallions, finely chopped
    Grated zest of 1/2 lemon
2   tablespoons fresh lemon juice
2   tablespoons chopped fresh thyme
    Chopped fresh parsley
    Minced scallion

Combine all ingredients except parsley and scallion in quart jar. Shake thoroughly. Chill overnight. Add parsley and scallion just before serving.

"CREAM" OF ZUCCHINI SOUP
MAKES 4 SERVINGS.

4   cups diced zucchini
2   cups Lite Way Chicken Stock (page 26) or 3 packets (1/2-1/2)
        chicken broth mixed with 2 cups water
3/4 cup chopped onion
1/4 cup diced celery
    Dash nutmeg
1   cup buttermilk

Combine all ingredients except buttermilk in saucepan. Heat to boiling; reduce heat and simmer, covered, 10 minutes or until onion and zucchini are very tender. Cool slightly. Purée in batches in blender until smooth. Return to saucepan; stir in buttermilk. Serve hot.

TOMATO VEGETABLE SOUP
MAKES 4 SERVINGS.

     1   cup diced celery
     2   cups fresh medium tomatoes, cored and chopped
    ³/₄ cup diced onion
    ¹/₂ cup diced carrot
 1 to 2 tablespoons chopped fresh basil, or ¹/₂ to 1 teaspoon dried
     3   cups Lite Way Chicken Stock (page 26)
    ¹/₂ cup plain yogurt
         Salt and pepper to taste

Combine celery, tomatoes, onion, carrot, and basil in medium saucepan; simmer 5 minutes. Add stock and simmer covered until vegetables are tender, about 10 minutes. Season with salt and pepper. Put soup through food mill or processor or blender. Add ¹/₂ cup plain yogurt. Serve cold or heat slowly to serve hot. Garnish with cubed peeled tomato bits and yogurt.

PUREE OF ASPARAGUS SOUP
MAKES 6 SERVINGS.

     1   pound asparagus, trimmed and blanched
     1   cup tomato juice
     3   cups stock or 3 packets instant beef broth + 1 cup water
    ¹/₄ teaspoon celery salt
    ¹/₄ teaspoon onion powder
         Pepper to taste

Purée asparagus, tomato juice, and stock in batches in blender until smooth. Pour into saucepan. Add remaining ingredients and simmer, covered, 20 minutes. Serve hot.

"CREAM" OF CAULIFLOWER SOUP
MAKES 6 SERVINGS.

> 2 cups stock or 2 packets instant chicken broth mixed with 2 cups water or 2 cups Lite Way Chicken Stock (page 26)
> 1 cup chopped celery
> 2 tablespoons grated onion
> 1/2 teaspoon salt
> Dash white pepper
> 3 cups chopped steamed cauliflower
> 1 1/2 cups evaporated skimmed milk
> Minced watercress or dash of paprika

Heat stock in saucepan to boiling. Add celery, onion, salt and pepper; cover and cook until celery is tender. Purée celery mixture in batches in blender until smooth. Add cauliflower in batches, pureeing after each addition until smooth. Return to saucepan; stir in milk and heat. Garnish each serving with watercress or paprika. Serve hot.

QUICK CLAM-VEGETABLE CHOWDER
MAKES 3 SERVINGS.

> 1 bottle (8 ounce) clam juice
> 1 can (10 1/2 ounce) minced clams, drained, liquid reserved
> 6 green onions or scallions, sliced
> 1 cup coarsely grated carrots
> 1/4 teaspoon dried thyme leaves
> 1/2 teaspoon salt
> 3/4 cup instant nonfat dry milk
> 1 cup Lite Way Stock (page 26)

Pour clam juice and liquid from minced clams into medium saucepan; cook about 10 minutes over medium heat. Reduce heat to moderately low; stir in green onions, carrots, thyme, and salt, cook 10 minutes more. Combine dry milk and soup stock; add to soup with drained clams and heat just until thoroughly heated.

EGG DROP SOUP
MAKES 1 SERVING.

>1 cup chicken bouillon or Lite Way Chicken Stock (page 26)
>1 medium egg, beaten
>1 small slice pared gingerroot, diced
>2 tablespoons scallion, including part of green top, chopped

Heat chicken bouillon to boiling; remove from heat. Stir the soup with a chopstick. With other hand, slowly pour the beaten egg into soup, stirring to create egg shreds. Remove from heat. Put ginger in soup bowl and add soup. Top with scallion. Serve at once.

SIZZLING MUSHROOM SOUP
MAKES 1 SERVING.

>3 dried mushrooms
>1 cup beef bouillon or Lite Way Chicken Stock (page 26)
>1/4 cup sherry or 1/2 teaspoon sherry extract
>1/2 cup chopped fresh or frozen spinach
>1 tablespoon chopped fresh parsley or chives

Rinse mushrooms in cold water. Combine stock and dried mushrooms in bowl. Let stand 15 minutes or until mushrooms are softened. Lift out mushrooms, rinse, cut away hard stems, and slice. Strain stock into saucepan and heat to boiling. Add sherry and mushroom slices. If using extract, add just before serving. Simmer, covered, for 20 minutes. Stir in spinach and cook 2 minutes more. Stir in parsley. Serve hot.

CHEESE AND EGGS

An overweight woman was overheard explaining her latest diet to a friend: "I eat nothing but vegetables and Zwieback, but of course I cover them in cheese so they'll taste good."

It is true cheese can make almost anything taste good. Unfortunately, many cheeses are high in fat and calories and are therefore taboo in the new lite eating patterns. Still, there are ways of keeping cheese on the menu as long as you select with care and watch the amounts.

GENERAL SUGGESTIONS FOR USING CHEESE

1. Use cheese with the lowest fat content whenever possible: dry curd, less than ½% milk fat cottage cheese; farmer cheese; pot cheese; Gammelöst; and Sapsago.

2. Use cheeses with medium fat content in moderation: St. Otho; Appenzeller Räss; Gjetost; Livarot; part-skim mozzarella; Parmesan; Reggiano; and Romano.

3. Avoid cheeses with high fat and salt content: cheddar; Jarlsberg; Muenster; Edam; Swiss; Gruyère; Port Salut; and Gouda.

4. Do not confuse low cholesterol with low fat cheeses. Swiss Chris and Swiss Lorraine, both low chloesterol, are as high in fats as Jarlsberg, brie, Gruyère and cheddar.

5. Use reduced calorie commercial cheeses that are clearly labeled as such; it can make a difference of as much as 70 calories per ounce.

6. Grated cheese goes further than sliced or cubed cheese and has fewer calories and salt per cup.

7. Make your own "cream cheese" according to the Lite Way recipe (page 172) —it has only 43 calories per ounce. Regular cream cheese has 106, while commercial imitation has 52.

8. Since soft cheese spreads more readily than hard cheese, it takes less to cover a cracker. That may mean fewer calories but processed cheeses are often high in salt and fat.

9. Hard cheeses are usually higher in fat content than higher moisture soft cheeses.

10. "Part skim" cheese is not necessarily lowfat cheese since milk and cream may have been added.

		Calories/ounce
Hard cheeses: American, Swiss, Romano		Over 110
Soft cheeses: cream cheese, Roquefort, blue		101–110
Cheese foods: American, Swiss, pimento		91–101
Cheese spreads: Neufchâtel, mozzarella, Limburger, Velveeta; Sapsago		75–90
Lite Way cheeses: farmer, cottage cheese, ricotta, pot, reduced calorie Gruyère type, or reduced calorie American type		0–50

½% fat cottage cheese	½ cup (4 ounce)	80
1% fat cottage cheese	½ cup (4 ounce)	90
2% fat cottage cheese	½ cup (4 ounce)	100
4% fat cottage cheese	½ cup (4 ounce)	120
Pot cheese	½ cup (4 ounce)	100
Whey cheese	½ cup (4 ounce)	80
Reduced calorie cheddar	1 ounce	50
Reduced calorie Gruyère	¾ ounce	35

Egg and Cheese Recipes

BAKED EGGS IN TOMATO SHELLS
MAKES 4 SERVINGS.

> 4 medium tomatoes
> Dash pepper
> Pinch dried basil
> Pinch dried oregano
> 4 eggs
> Parsley sprigs

Cut off top of tomato ¼ of the way down. Scoop out the pulp and save for other uses. Drain tomatoes on paper towels. Sprinkle the inside of each with pepper, oregano, and basil. Break eggs, one at a time, into a small dish and gently slip one into each shell. Place tomatoes in shallow baking pan. Bake in 350° oven for 20 to 25 minutes or until eggs are as "set" as you prefer. Garnish with fresh parsley.

INDIVIDUAL MUSHROOM SCALLION QUICHE
MAKES 6 SERVINGS.

3 or 4	scallions, thinly sliced
1	cup sliced mushrooms
1/2	cup Lite Way Chicken Stock (page 26)
4	eggs, lightly beaten
2	cups milk
1/4	teaspoon nutmeg
1/4	teaspoon white pepper
1	tablespoon grated Parmesan cheese

Simmer scallions and mushrooms in broth in saucepan until tender, about 3-4 minutes. Combine with eggs, milk, nutmeg, pepper, and cheese in bowl. Pour into 6 small ramekins (sprayed with vegetable cooking spray) and place ramekins in pan containing 1/2-inch hot water. Bake in 350° oven until knife inserted in center comes out clean, about 25 minutes.

FLUFFY OMELET
MAKES 2 SERVINGS.

3	eggs, separated
1	cup plain lowfat yogurt
1/3	cup regular wheat germ
3	tablespoons minced fresh parsley
3/4	teaspoon rosemary leaves, crushed
1/2	teaspoon salt
	Tomato wedges
	Blanched snow peas
	Sautéed sliced mushrooms

Combine egg yolks, yogurt, wheat germ, parsley, rosemary, and salt in small bowl. Beat egg whites in separate bowl until very stiff peaks form. Fold whites into egg yolk mixture. Pour into 9-inch oven-proof skillet sprayed with vegetable cooking spray. Bake in 350° oven for 15 to 18 minutes or until set. Loosen edges of omelet with spatula. Tip pan and fold omelet in half. Invert onto serving plate. Top with tomato wedges, blanched snow peas, and sliced mushrooms, as desired.

NO CRUST CHEESE AND SPINACH PIE

MAKES 4-6 SERVINGS.

Serve for lunch or as an appetizer.

- 1 package (10 ounces) spinach
- 1 pound part-skim ricotta cheese
- 6 ounces part-skim grated mozzarella cheese
- 3 eggs, lightly beaten
- 1 teaspoon onion powder or garlic powder or
  1 tablespoon minced onion or 1 teaspoon minced garlic
- 1 teaspoon dill, fresh or dry
- 1 teaspoon salt
- 1/2 teaspoon pepper

Optional (choose preferences):

Simmer vegetable of choice in broth 5-7 minutes until slightly tender.

- 1/2 cup Lite Way Stock (page 26) or bouillon
- 1 cup zucchini, sliced
- 1/2 cup green pepper, cut coarsely
- 1/2 cup ham cut in small pieces
- 1 cup broccoli cut coarsely
- 1/2 cup onions chopped
- 1/2 cup mushrooms quartered

Heat 3/4 cup water in saucepan to boiling. Add spinach and cover pan, cook about 5 minutes, then drain spinach in colander or strainer; squeeze out water. Combine spinach, ricotta cheese, grated mozzarella cheese, eggs, seasonings, and vegetables, if using, in a large bowl. Pour mixture into 9- or 10-inch nonstick pan, quiche dish, or deep pie plate sprayed with vegetable cooking spray. Bake in 350° oven for about 40 minutes until set. Middle may not be quite firm. Let stand 10 minutes.

CHEESE OMELET

MAKES 2 SERVINGS.

- 4 eggs, separated
- 2 ounces grated Sapsago or part-skim mozzarella cheese
- 1/4 cup evaporated skimmed milk
- 1/2 teaspoon salt

Beat egg whites until stiff but not dry. Combine egg yolks, cheese, milk, and salt in medium bowl. Fold into the beaten whites. Pour mixture into 9- or 10-inch preheated nonstick skillet sprayed with vegetable cooking spray. Cook over low heat, lifting edges of egg as they set and tilting skillet so uncooked egg flows underneath. When underside is just set, flip omelet and brown second side. Serve in wedges.

SCRAMBLED EGGS WITH BROCCOLI
MAKES 2 SERVINGS.

      4   eggs
    1/4   cup skim milk
    1/4   teaspoon salt
          Dash paprika
          Dash Tabasco
    1/2   cooked chopped broccoli, well drained
    1/4   cup low fat cottage cheese

Lightly beat eggs with milk, salt, paprika, and Tabasco in medium bowl. Stir in broccoli and cheese. Pour egg mixture into medium skillet prepared with vegetable spray. Cook, stirring occasionally, over low heat until eggs are set but still slightly moist.

MUSHROOM-ASPARAGUS OPEN OMELET
MAKES 2 SERVINGS.

      4   eggs
    1/2   cup steamed, chopped asparagus tips, drained
    1/2   cup cooked sliced mushrooms, drained
      1   teaspoon water or vegetable cooking liquid
    1/4   teaspoon salt
          Pepper to taste.

Beat eggs in bowl until frothy. Stir in remaining ingredients. Pour into preheated nonstick skillet. Cook over moderate heat. As mixture sets, lift up edges and tilt skillet so uncooked egg flows underneath. When underside is set, about 2 minutes, flip with spatula. Cook until the bottom is set and golden brown, about 2 minutes.

BACO-CHEESE OMELET
MAKES 1 SERVING.

        1 egg
        1 tablespoon water
           Salt and pepper to taste
        1 tablespoon imitation bacon chips
        1 tablespoon part-skim mozzarella, grated

Beat egg with water in small bowl. Pour into nonstick pan sprayed with vegetable cooking spray. Cook over medium heat until mixture sets. Sprinkle "bacon chips" and grated cheese on omelet. Fold omelet over. Let cheese melt.

ORANGE NOG
MAKES 1 SERVING.

        1 egg
       ½ cup orange juice
        2 tablespoons skim milk
           Dash nutmeg

Blend ingredients in blender until smooth. Serve cold.

EGG CUP
MAKES 1 SERVING.

        1 egg
        1 slice very thin whole grain bread

Remove and discard crust from bread. Place bread in nonstick muffin tin to form cup. Bake until brown. Drop in 1 egg. Season to taste. Bake in 350° oven for 20 to 25 minutes or until egg sets.

CREAMY CHEESE BAKED EGG
MAKES 1 SERVING.

        1 tablespoon plain lowfat yogurt
        1 tablespoon Lite Way Sour Cream #1 (page 172)
        1 large egg
        2 tablespoons grated part-skim mozzarella or Sapsago
              cheese

Heat oven to 400°. In small bowl mix yogurt and Lite Way sour cream. Spray an 8-ounce custard cup with vegetable cooking spray. Break egg into prepared cup, top with yogurt mixture, and sprinkle with cheese. Bake 10 to 12 minutes in regular oven or 8 to 9 minutes in toaster oven, or until egg has set and cheese has melted.

COTTAGE CHEESE PANCAKES
MAKES 8 PANCAKES.

     1   cup lowfat cottage cheese
     1   egg
     1/2 cup flour
     1/2 teaspoon baking powder
     1/4 teaspoon salt

Blend all ingredients in medium bowl until well combined. Drop batter from a spoon onto pan with nonstick surface. Cook over medium heat until lightly browned. Turn once.

CHEESE DANISH
MAKES 1 SERVING.

     1   slice toast
     1   teaspoon low-calorie jam or cinnamon
     1/4 cup lowfat cottage cheese or whey cheese.

Spread jam and cheese on toast. Bake at 400° for 3 minutes in toaster or regular oven until cheese bubbles.

BAGEL POWER
MAKES 1 SERVING.

     1/2 toasted dugout bagel
     3/4 ounce cut up reduced calorie "Gruyère type" cheese or 1
          ounce cut up part-skim mozzarella.

Place cheese on toasted bagel. Broil in regular oven or toaster oven until cheese bubbles and browns slightly (3-5 min.).

CHEESE PITA
MAKES 1 SERVING.

  1   ounce part-skim mozzarella, sliced
  ½   whole wheat 7 inch pita bread (split horizontally)

Place cheese on pita. Broil until cheese bubbles (3-5 min.).

BAKED EGGPLANT PARMIGIANA
MAKES 2 SERVINGS.

  ¼   cup chopped onion
  ¼   cup chicken or veal stock
  ¾   cup tomato purée
  ⅓   cup water
  ¾   teaspoon salt
  ½   teaspoon dried oregano leaves
      Dash pepper
  2   cups peeled and thinly sliced eggplant
  4   ounces grated Mozzarella cheese

In nonstick skillet, brown chopped onion in stock 3-5 minutes. Add tomato purée, water, salt, oregano, and pepper. Heat to boiling and simmer for 15 minutes. In 2-quart baking dish, layer half the sliced eggplant, half the tomato sauce, and half the grated cheese; repeat layer of eggplant and tomato sauce. Bake in 350° oven for 1 hour. A few minutes before done, sprinkle remaining grated cheese over top and continue baking until cheese melts.

EGGPLANT ITALIANO
MAKES 4 SERVINGS.

        1   pound canned or fresh tomatoes
        1   can (8 ounces) tomato sauce
        ¼   cup chopped celery
        ¼   cup sliced onion
¼ to ½   teaspoon salt
          Dash sweetener
        ¼   teaspoon dried oregano leaves
        ¼   teaspoon dried basil leaves
        ⅛   teaspoon rubbed sage
          Dash pepper

1 eggplant (about 1 pound), sliced into ½-inch slices
1 cup cottage cheese or part-skim ricotta cheese
2 tablespoons grated Parmesan cheese
¼ pound part-skim mozzarella cheese, sliced

Combine the tomatoes, tomato sauce, celery, onion, and seasonings in a saucepan. Simmer, uncovered, over medium heat for 30 minutes. Meanwhile, cook eggplant slices in a little boiling water for about 5 minutes; drain well. In a 1½-quart rectangular baking dish layer the tomato sauce, eggplant, and cottage cheese. Sprinkle with Parmesan cheese. Top with mozzarella slices. Bake uncovered, in 425° oven 10 minutes, or until cheese is lightly browned and mixture is heated through.

PITA SANDWICH

MAKES 1 SERVING.

½ whole wheat 7-inch pita bread (split horizontally)
2 ounces part-skim mozzarella, sliced thin
  Alfalfa sprouts (optional)
5 cucumber slices
2 tomato slices
1 teaspoon imitation bacon bits
  Lemon Pepper Seasoning (page 24)
1 teaspoon prepared mustard

Spread mustard in pita pocket and layer cheese, sprouts, cucumber, and tomato. Sprinkle with bacon bits. Sprinkle lightly with Lemon Pepper seasoning.

VEGETARIAN'S DELIGHT

MAKES 4 SERVINGS.

1 cup onion, chopped
2 cloves garlic, pressed through garlic press
2 cups zucchini, sliced
1 cup broth
3 eggs, beaten
1 cup lowfat cottage cheese
½ cup nonfat dry milk powder
½ teaspoon garlic powder
¼ cup shredded part-skim mozzarella

Cook onion and garlic in ¹/₂ cup broth until tender. Add zucchini and additional broth and cook about 10 minutes. Cool slightly. Spoon vegetable mixture into 9-by-9-inch dish sprayed with vegetable cooking spray. Mix eggs, cheese, milk and garlic powder together. Pour over vegetables. Bake in 375° oven 40 minutes. Sprinkle with shredded cheese. Bake 5 more minutes, or until cheese melts.

STUFFED PITA
MAKES 1 SERVING.

- ¹/₂ cup chopped asparagus, or green beans, or broccoli
- ¹/₂ cup chopped tomatoes
- 1 tablespoon alfalfa sprouts
- 1 teaspoon chopped shallots
- ¹/₂ teaspoon basil
  Cayenne to taste
- ¹/₂ pita bread, 7-inches (cut in half to form pocket)
- ¹/₄ cup grated Sapsago cheese

Steam green vegetable until crisp-tender. Drain well. Mix with tomato, sprouts, and seasonings in medium bowl. Stuff into pita and sprinkle with cheese. Heat in 350° oven until cheese melts. Serve immediately.

CHEESE AND SPINACH TORTE
MAKES 4 SERVINGS.

- ¹/₂ pound fresh spinach, trimmed, washed
- 4 eggs
- 1 cup part-skim ricotta cheese or low-fat cottage cheese
- 1 cup skim milk
- 3 tablespoons grated Parmesan cheese
- 1 tablespoon Dijon-style mustard
- ¹/₂ teaspoon Italian Seasoning (page 24)
  Salt and pepper to taste
- 1 teaspoon oil

Cook spinach in boiling water until tender, about 2 minutes. Drain, squeeze excess moisture from spinach, and chop. Makes about ¹/₂ cup. Beat eggs lightly in bowl. Add ricotta; mix well. Stir in milk, a little at a time, until smooth. Add spinach, Parmesan cheese, mustard, seasonings; mix well. Oil 4 individual ramekins. Spoon in filling and smooth the tops. Bake in 450° oven for 15 minutes.

SALADS and SALAD DRESSINGS

Salads are the perfect food for eating the Lite Way: the ingredients are high in bulk and water, free of starch, sugar, and fats (as long as you watch the dressings), and as varied as your imagination can make them. Anyone who considers salads boring has not explored their possibilities:

- There are 22 different kinds of lettuce to provide variety.
- There are 4 kinds of sprouts to give salad added interest.
- There are raw vegetables—cauliflower, broccoli, zucchini, mushrooms, and spinach—to furnish added texture.
- There are vegetables you may never have even tried—Jerusalem artichokes and endive, for instance.

A word of warning: what you put in a salad can turn an innocent lettuce leaf into a high calorie weapon. You must be careful. Look for low calorie alternatives to the high calorie goodies you are accustomed to:

Goodies with High Calories		Low Calorie Substitutes	
1 teaspoon crumbled bacon	70	1 teaspoon Baco Bits	25
3 ounces marinated artichokes	90	3 ounces canned artichoke hearts	35
4 walnuts	100	4 water chestnuts	20
1 cup avocado	260	1 cup alfalfa sprouts	40
1/2 cup croutons	80	1/2 cup bean sprouts	25

43

What you put *on* a salad can make or break the calorie count as well. Commercial diet dressings ease the situation by as much as 90 calories per tablespoon. Lite Way recipes offer a wide variety of oil-less salad dressings using lowfat yogurt, buttermilk, and puréed vegetables as substitutes.

GENERAL SUGGESTIONS FOR LITE WAY SALADS AND DRESSINGS

1. Experiment with new kinds of raw vegetables for added variety.
2. Try a salad of chilled undercooked vegetables.
3. Marinate mushrooms and zucchini in vinegar and herbs before adding them to a salad.
4. Add a small amount of drained, water-packed tuna to a salad.
5. Sprinkle grated Parmesan cheese over salad.
6. Add crunch to a salad with water chestnuts, sprouts, and imitation bacon bits.
7. Make your own mayonnaise the Lite Way.
8. Serve raw vegetables with low-calorie dressing as a dip.
9. Add powdered salad dressings to plain lowfat yogurt instead of to oil and vinegar.
10. Add pieces of reduced calorie cheese to a salad.
11. Add leftover cooked chicken or turkey to a salad.
12. Have you tried . . .

Greens
Butterhead lettuce
Beet, collard, or
turnip greens
Endive or sorrel

Cabbages
Red
Savoy
Chinese

Celery
Bok Choy
Fennel

Squash
Spaghetti squash
Scalloped squash
Chayote squash

Onions
Leeks
Shallots

Others
Kohlrabi
Rutabaga
Celeriac
Salsify
Jerusalem artichoke

SALAD NIÇOISE
MAKES 4 SERVINGS.

   2   cups fresh or frozen green beans, trimmed, cooked
           al dente, and cooled
   3   tomatoes, cored, quartered
   1   head red-leafed lettuce, shredded
   4   scallions, chopped
   1   can (7½ ounces) water-packed tuna
   1   sliced hard-boiled egg
      Pimentos (optional)
      Bell pepper rings (optional)
 ½   cup Lite Italian Dressing (page 62)

Toss beans, tomatoes, lettuce, scallions, and tuna in a large bowl. Garnish with egg slices and the pimento and bell pepper rings, if desired. Add dressing. Toss well.

CUCUMBERS IN YOGURT-DILL SAUCE
MAKES 2 SERVINGS.

   1   cup thinly sliced cucumber
 ½   teaspoon salt
 ½   cup thinly sliced onion
 ¼   cup plain lowfat yogurt
   1   tablespoon chopped fresh dill or 1 teaspoon dried dill
   1   tablespoon sliced scallion
   1   tablespoon cider vinegar

Combine cucumbers and salt in a medium bowl; stir and set aside. Combine remaining ingredients in a medium bowl. Drain cucumber slices, rinse, and pat dry with paper towels. Add yogurt mixture to cucumber slices in serving bowl and toss to combine. Cover and chill about 1 hour to blend flavors.

BROCCOLI-TOMATO SALAD
MAKES 2 SERVINGS.

    2   cups coarsely chopped broccoli
    2   green onions, chopped
    1   tomato, peeled, diced

Bring broccoli to boil in 2 cups of water. Cover and let broccoli cook without heat only until still crisp, but tender. Rinse with cold water; drain. Combine broccoli with green onion and tomato in a medium bowl. Chill, covered. Add ¼ cup Herbed Yogurt dressing and toss well.

ZUCCHINI SALAD
MAKES 4 SERVINGS.

    1   cup plain lowfat yogurt
    4   tablespoons chopped fresh mint leaves or 1 tablespoon
            dried mint
    1   tablespoon fresh lemon juice
    2   cups thinly sliced zucchini
        Lettuce leaves

Combine yogurt, mint, and lemon juice in a medium bowl. Add zucchini and toss. Chill, covered. Serve on lettuce leaves.

CHEF'S SALAD
MAKES 1 SERVING.

        Lettuce leaves
    2   ounces julienned cooked chicken (white meat) or turkey,
            or 3 ounces drained water-packed tuna, or 4 ounces
            boiled shrimp
    ½   tomato
    ½   ounce grated Sapsago cheese
        Cucumber slices
        Mushroom slices
        Grated carrot

Arrange lettuce leaves on a plate. Arrange chicken, turkey, tuna, or shrimp on lettuce with tomato, grated cheese, cucumbers, mushroom slices, and grated carrot. Add one of the dressings.

Dressing: Fresh lemon juice or vinegar or 2 tablespoons plain lowfat yogurt mixed with chopped fresh dill.

CHICKEN AND BEAN SPROUT SALAD
MAKES 4 SERVINGS.

1	tablespoon soy sauce
2	teaspoons wine vinegar
2	teaspoons vegetable oil
1/2	teaspoon sugar
2 1/4	cups sliced cooked chicken
4	cups bean sprouts, rinsed, drained

Combine soy sauce, vinegar, oil, and sugar in a small bowl. Combine chicken and bean sprouts in another bowl; add to dressing and toss. Serve well chilled.

CRUNCHY HAWAIIAN TURKEY SALAD
MAKES 4 SERVINGS.

2 1/2	cups cubed cooked turkey
1/2	cup Tangy Hawaiian Dressing (page 61)
1/2	cup sliced celery
1/2	cup pineapple chunks
1/4	cup sliced water chestnuts
1/2	teaspoon sugar
1/4	teaspoon Italian Seasoning (page 24)
1/8	teaspoon ground ginger
3	cups finely shredded lettuce
	Watercress
	Poppy seeds

Marinate turkey in Tangy Hawaiian Dressing in refrigerator several hours or overnight. Drain, reserving 1/4 cup dressing. In large bowl, toss marinated turkey, reserved dressing, the celery, pineapple, water chestnuts, and seasonings. Serve over lettuce. Garnish with watercress and sprinkle poppy seeds over all.

CURRIED CHICKEN SALAD

MAKES FOUR 4-OUNCE SERVINGS.

2	whole chicken breasts
1/2	cup plain lowfat yogurt
1/4	teaspoon curry powder
1/4	teaspoon ground ginger
2	scallions, thinly sliced
3	tablespoons coarsely chopped green pepper
1/2	cup drained water-packed pineapple chunks
2	tablespoons raisins
1/4	teaspoon salt
	Romaine lettuce
	Radish rose

Poach chicken in a large skillet in water enough to cover over low heat until tender, about 45 minutes. Remove chicken from broth and chill. Refrigerate poaching liquid or freeze for other use. When chicken is cold, remove and discard bones and skin. Cut meat into bite-size pieces. Mix remaining ingredients together in a bowl. Add chicken pieces and mix well. Refrigerate, covered. Serve chilled on romaine lettuce leaves. Garnish with a radish rose.

JAPANESE SHRIMP SALAD

MAKES 2 SERVINGS.

1	cup shredded lettuce
1/4	fresh medium pineapple
2	teaspoons fresh lemon juice
1	small orange, peeled, sectioned
2	medium tomatoes, sliced
1/4	cup plain lowfat yogurt
4	ounces cooked shrimp or cooked chicken, cubed

Make a bed of greens on two chilled salad plates. Peel and core pineapple quarter. Slice fruit into small triangular segments. Sprinkle with lemon juice. Arrange half the pineapple, orange sections, and tomato slices in a circle on the lettuce on each plate. Place one-half of the yogurt in middle of each circle. Add shrimp.

ITALIAN ZUCCHINI SALAD
MAKES 4 SERVINGS.

- 4 cups sliced zucchini (4 small zucchini)
- ½ cup sour pickle relish
- ¼ cup vinegar
  Artificial sweetener to equal 2 teaspoons sugar
- ½ teaspoon salt
  Pepper to taste
- 1 cup cherry tomatoes
- ½ cup sliced celery
- ¼ head lettuce, torn into pieces

Marinate zucchini with relish, vinegar, and seasonings in medium bowl in refrigerator for at least 2 hours. Stir occasionally. Toss zucchini and marinade with other ingredients in large bowl. Serve chilled.

CARROT SALAD
MAKES 4 SERVINGS.

- 2 cups coarsely grated or chopped carrots (about 3 medium)
- 2 tablespoons chopped fresh parsley
- 2 tablespoons sliced scallions or green onions
- 1½ tablespoons cider vinegar
- ½ tablespoon vegetable oil
- ½ teaspoon salt
  Black pepper to taste

Put all ingredients in a bowl and toss to blend. Serve chilled.

TOMATO, ONION, AND SHRIMP SALAD
MAKES 1 SERVING.

  Lettuce leaves
- 1 medium tomato, sliced
- 3 thin slices Spanish onion
- 1½ teaspoons chopped fresh parsley
- 1 teaspoon vegetable oil
- ½ teaspoon Dijon-style mustard
- ¼ teaspoon dried basil, oregano, or thyme
  Pepper to taste
- 3½ ounces cooked shrimp

Place lettuce on plate. Arrange alternating rings of tomatoes and onions on lettuce. Combine remaining ingredients except shrimp in small bowl and pour over tomatoes and onions. Arrange shrimp on plate. Let stand a few minutes before serving.

CHINESE SALAD WITH SHRIMP
MAKES 1 SERVING.

- 1 head Chinese cabbage, chopped
- 2 hard-boiled eggs, chopped
- 1 can (4 ounces) shrimp, drained, chopped
- 1 tablespoon Lite Way Mayonnaise #1 (page 178)
- ½ teaspoon dry mustard

Combine cabbage, eggs, and shrimp in a bowl. Combine mayonnaise with mustard in small bowl. Add dressing to cabbage mixture and toss well.

TOMATO-SHRIMP MOUSSE
MAKES 4 SERVINGS.

- 1 envelope unflavored gelatin
- ¼ cup cold water
- ½ cup evaporated skimmed milk
- 4 medium tomatoes, peeled, seeded, chopped
- 1 cup tomato purée
- 2 teaspoons fresh lemon juice
  Salt and cayenne pepper to taste
- 12 ounces cooked shrimp
  Lettuce leaves

Sprinkle gelatin over water in blender container or food processer to soften, about 5 minutes. Scald skimmed milk in small saucepan. Pour into blender and process. Cook chopped tomato with tomato purée in medium saucepan until soft. Season with lemon juice, salt and pepper. Let cool. Add tomato mixture and shrimp to blender. (*Note:* This may have to be done in batches.) Pour purée into four individual molds and chill for 2 hours or until set. Unmold and serve on bed of lettuce leaves on four chilled plates.

MELON AND SHRIMP COCKTAIL
MAKES 2 SERVINGS.

- ½ ripe cantaloupe, seeded, cubed or balled
- 7 ounces cooked shrimp
  Lite Way Cocktail Sauce (page 62)
  Lemon wedges

Combine melon and shrimp in medium bowl. Spoon into 2 serving bowls. Top each serving with 1 tablespoon of cocktail sauce. Garnish with lemon wedges.

CRABMEAT SALAD
MAKES 3 SERVINGS.

- 18 canned or cooked asparagus spears, drained
- 1 tablespoon Italian Dressing (page 62)
- 1 can (7 ounces) crabmeat, drained, flaked
- ½ cup chopped celery
- ¾ teaspoon minced onion
- ½ teaspoon prepared horseradish
- 1 teaspoon fresh lemon juice
- 3 tablespoons Lite Way Mayonnaise (page 178)
- 6 large lettuce leaves
- 3 hard-boiled eggs, halved
- 1 medium cucumber, cut into spears
- 3 green onions or scallions
- 6 tomato slices
  Watercress (optional)

Sprinkle asparagus with Italian Lite Way dressing; toss to coat, and chill about 1 hour. Mix together in medium bowl the crabmeat, celery, onion, horseradish, lemon juice and Lite Way mayonnaise. Line 3 plates with 2 lettuce leaves on each. Arrange on each lettuce bed 6 asparagus spears, ½ cup crabmeat salad, 2 egg halves, one third of the cucumber spears, 1 green onion, and 2 tomato slices. Garnish with a sprig of watercress, if desired.

TUNA AND ALFALFA SPROUTS
MAKES 1 SERVING.

> 1   can (3½ ounces) water-packed tuna, drained, flaked
>   Small handful of alfalfa sprouts
> 2   tomato slices
> 1   teaspoon imitation bacon bits
> 1   thin slice whole wheat bread or ½ whole wheat 7-inch pita
>   bread (split horizontally or cut across center)

Layer tuna, sprouts, and tomatoes on bread, pita half, or into pita pouch. Sprinkle with bacon bits.

MIXED SALMON SALAD
MAKES 4 SERVINGS.

> 1   cup thinly sliced small mushrooms
> ½   head iceburg lettuce, chopped
> ½   head romaine, chopped
> 1   bunch watercress, chopped
> 10   cherry tomatoes, cut in halves
> 8   radishes, sliced
> 14   ounces salmon
> ½   cup Lite Creamy Dill dressing (page 59)

Combine all ingredients in large bowl. Toss and divide into 4 equal portions. Serve with dressing.

SALMON STUFFED TOMATO
MAKES 4 SERVINGS.

> 4   medium tomatoes
> 1   can (1 pound) salmon, drained, flaked
> ½   cup diced celery
> ¼   cup finely chopped green pepper
> 1   tablespoon minced onion
> 1   tablespoon toasted sesame seeds
> 2   teaspoons fresh lemon juice
> ⅛   teaspoon dry mustard
> 3   tablespoons Lite Way Mayonnaise (page 178)
>   Salt and pepper to taste
> 2   hard-boiled eggs

Cut a thin slice from top of each tomato and scoop out most of interior. Invert tomatoes on a plate to drain while making salad. Mix together in a large bowl the salmon, celery, green pepper, onion, sesame seeds, lemon juice, mustard, Lite Way mayonnaise, and salt and pepper. Sieve 1 cooked egg yolk and reserve; chop remaining eggs and stir into salmon mixture. Stuff each tomato with one-fourth of mixture. Garnish top of each with some of the sieved reserved yolk.

SUPER SPINACH
MAKES 2 SERVINGS.

- 1 package fresh spinach, washed
- 1 cup mushrooms, sliced
- 1/4 pound raw cauliflower, broken into flowerets
- 1 small yellow crookneck squash, sliced
- 3 hard-boiled eggs
- 3 tablespoons imitation bacon bits

Combine all ingredients in bowl. Season to taste.

CHEF'S SALAD
MAKES 1 SERVING.

- 1 cup shredded lettuce
- 1/2 cup sliced mushrooms
- 1/4 medium green pepper, diced
- 1/4 cup cubed cooked turkey
- 1/4 cup onion, sliced
- 1 pimento, cut into strips
- 1 hard-boiled egg, chopped
- 1 ounce part-skim mozzarella cheese, cubed
- 2 tablespoons evaporated skimmed milk
- 1 tablespoon Lite Way Mayonnaise #1 (page 178)
- 2 tablespoons fresh lemon juice
- 1 teaspoon chopped capers
    Salt and pepper to taste

Combine lettuce, mushrooms, green pepper, turkey, onion, and pimento in large salad bowl. Toss in egg and cheese. In small mixing bowl, combine remaining ingredients. Pour over salad and mix.

EGG SALAD OR TUNA STUFFED TOMATO
MAKES 1 SERVING.

    1   medium tomato
    2   hard-boiled eggs, chopped, or 2 ounces water-packed tuna
          fish, drained, flaked
   ¼   cup low-fat cottage cheese
1 to 2   tablespoons chopped onion, green pepper, chives, or radish
       Salt and pepper to taste

Cut a thin slice from top of tomato. Scoop out interior, and invert tomato on plate to drain. Mix remaining ingredients in a bowl. Spoon stuffing into tomato.

CHICKEN SALAD PLATTER WITH TOMATO WEDGES AND HARD-BOILED EGG
MAKES 4 SERVINGS.

    1   cup cubed cooked chicken
   ¼   cup instant onion
    1   stalk celery, diced
  1½   tablespoons Lite Way Mayonnaise #1 (page 178)
    2   teaspoons fresh lemon juice
    1   teaspoon salt
    1   teaspoon chopped fresh parsley
       Lettuce leaves
    2   tomatoes, cut in wedges
    2   hard-boiled eggs, halved

Combine chicken, onion, celery, Lite Way mayonnaise, lemon juice, and salt in bowl. Mix well; chill. Arrange a bed of lettuce on four plates. Spoon salad on each plate. Sprinkle each with parsley and garnish with tomato wedges and egg halves.

ORIENTAL CHICKEN OR TUNA SALAD
MAKES 2 SERVINGS.

    1   cup bean sprouts, drained, washed
    1   cup diced cooked chicken or drained, flaked water-packed
          tuna
   ½   cup water chestnuts, drained, sliced

¹/₂ cup sliced celery
¹/₄ cup chopped green pepper
1 cup fresh or 1 can (4 ounces) sliced mushrooms, drained
2 cups raw spinach leaves, washed, torn into bite-size pieces
¹/₄ head lettuce, torn into bite-size pieces

Combine all ingredients in large salad bowl. Add one of the Lite Way Dressings (pp. 58–63) if desired.

Side Dish Salads

COLE SLAW
MAKES 4-6 SERVINGS.

³/₄ cup buttermilk
¹/₃ cup cider vinegar
¹/₂ teaspoon dry mustard
Salt and pepper to taste
3 cups shredded cabbage
Dash artificial sweetener

Blend buttermilk with vinegar in large bowl. Add mustard, salt, pepper, and sweetener. Add cabbage and toss well. For variety, try curry powder or chili powder to taste.

TARRAGON CUCUMBERS
MAKES 2 SERVINGS.

¹/₄ cup cider vinegar
¹/₄ cup water
Artificial sweetener to equal 2 teaspoons sugar
¹/₂ teaspoon dried tarragon
¹/₄ teaspoon salt
¹/₈ teaspoon garlic powder
2 cups sliced pared cucumbers

Combine all ingredients except cucumbers in medium bowl. Add cucumbers; toss to coat. Chill, covered, at least 2 hours. Toss before serving.

STRING BEAN SALAD
MAKES 2 SERVINGS.

> 1 cup fresh green beans, washed, trimmed, and broken into pieces
> 1 teaspoon tarragon vinegar
> 1/2 teaspoon dry mustard
> 1/2 clove garlic, finely chopped
> Boston lettuce leaves

Steam beans over boiling water for 2 to 3 minutes until crisp-tender. Drain in colander and run under cold water to cool. Place beans in serving bowl. Combine vinegar, mustard, and garlic in small bowl. Pour mixture over beans and toss to coat. Refrigerate, covered, at least 1 hour. Toss before serving. Arrange beans on Boston lettuce leaves on individual plates.

SWEET 'N SOUR CUCUMBERS
MAKES 6-8 SERVINGS.

> 2 large cucumbers, thinly sliced
> 1/4 teaspoon salt
> 1 large onion, sliced
> Dash white pepper
> 1/2 cup white vinegar
> 2 tablespoons water
> Artificial sweetener to equal 1/4 cup

Sprinkle cucumbers in colander with salt and let stand 30 minutes. Rinse and dry with paper towels. Combine cucumber and onions in medium bowl. Sprinkle with pepper. Combine vinegar, water, and sweetener in small bowl, and pour over cucumbers and onions. Toss to combine and marinate at least 3 hours before serving. May be stored in tight jar.

RAW VEGETABLE PLATE
MAKES 4 SERVINGS.

> 4 leaves Bibb lettuce
> 1 cup string beans, trimmed
> 1 cup cauliflower flowerets
> 1/2 cup sliced mushrooms

> 4   whole scallions
> 4   thin strips of zucchini
> 1/2 cup plain lowfat yogurt
>   Snipped fresh chives
>   Fresh lemon juice

Place lettuce leaves on 4 plates. Arrange raw vegetables on leaves.
Combine yogurt, chives, and lemon juice in small bowl; use as dip
for vegetables.

CHINESE SALAD
MAKES 4 SERVINGS.

> 1   pound fresh bean sprouts or 1 can sprouts, washed, rinsed
>   in cold water at least 3 times, drained
>   Strips of cooked chicken or turkey (optional)
> 6   scallions cut into thin strips
> 2   tablespoons sesame seeds
> 1/2 cup soy sauce

Combine first four ingredients in large bowl. Pour soy sauce over
salad and toss to combine.

CABBAGE-CARROT SALAD
MAKES 4 SERVINGS.

> 3/4   pound cabbage, cut into thin strips
> 1 1/2 medium carrots, finely grated
> 1/2   cup unsweetened or fresh pineapple, cut into thin strips
>   Fruit Dressing

Combine cabbage, carrot, and pineapple in large bowl. Add Fruit
Dressing (1/4 cup Lite Way Mayonnaise, page 178, mixed with 1/4
cup pineapple juice) and toss to combine.

BEET AND ENDIVE SALAD
MAKES 8 SERVINGS.

 4   heads Belgian endive, sliced lengthwise
 ¼   head lettuce, torn into bite-size pieces
 2   cups canned drained julienne-style beets
 1   cup sliced celery
 1   medium onion, cut into rings
     Watercress leaves

Combine all ingredients together in large bowl, add dressing.

Dressing the Lite Way

MAYONNAISE DRESSINGS
Start with:

 1   cup imitation mayonnaise or Lite Way mayonnaise (p. 178)
       or
 1   cup plain lowfat yogurt mixed with 1 tablespoon imitation
       or regular mayonnaise

Add:
1. *Dill* (Makes about 1⅓ cups)

 ⅓   cup snipped fresh dill
 1   tablespoon Dijon-style mustard
 1   teaspoon anchovy paste
 1   mashed garlic clove

2. *Thousand Island* (Makes about 1¼ cups)

 2   tablespoons chili sauce
 1   tablespoon minced green onion
 ½   teaspoon minced pimento
 ½   teaspoon snipped fresh chives

3. *Niçoise* (Makes about 1¼ cups)

¼   cup tomato purée
1   green or red pepper, chopped
¼   teaspoon minced fresh or dried tarragon
¼   teaspoon snipped fresh chives

Cook tomato purée in small saucepan over medium heat until liquid evaporates. Cool. Combine with remaining ingredients.

RUSSIAN DRESSINGS
MAKES ABOUT 1½ CUPS.

½   cup tomato juice
¼   cup diced peeled tomato
1   tablespoon tomato sauce
          OR
½   cup tomato purée
¼   cup snipped fresh chives, green or red pepper, pimento, onion, and/or scallion, chopped
1   cup Lite Way Mayonnaise (page 178) or Lite Way Sour Cream (page 172) or imitation mayonnaise

Mix the tomato juice or tomato purée combination of ingredients with the Lite Way mayonnaise, sour cream, or imitation mayonnaise. Refrigerate, covered, until ready to use.

CREAMY DILL DRESSING
MAKES ABOUT 1 CUP.

1   cup fat-free cottage cheese
2   tablespoons skim milk
1   tablespoon fresh lemon juice
1   teaspoon dill weed
½   teaspoon celery salt
⅛   teaspoon grated lemon

Process all the ingredients in blender or food processor until smooth. Refrigerate, covered, until ready to use.

CREAMY LEMON AND GARLIC DRESSING
MAKES ABOUT 1 CUP.

2/3	cup buttermilk
3	tablespoons fresh lemon juice
3	tablespoons water
4 1/2	teaspoons minced fresh parsley
1/2	teaspoon grated lemon zest
1/2	teaspoon dry mustard
1/2	teaspoon sugar
1/2	teaspoon Lemon Pepper Seasoning (page 24)
1/2	teaspoon garlic powder
1/4	teaspoon dillweed
1/4	teaspoon turmeric
1/4	teaspoon seasoned pepper

In jar with tight-fitting lid, shake all ingredients until blended. Chill, covered, several hours to blend flavors.

TARRAGON DRESSING
MAKES ABOUT 1 CUP.

1/4	cup coarsely chopped onion
1	clove garlic
3/4	cup Lite Way Chicken Stock (page 26)
1/4	cup tarragon vinegar
1	egg yolk
1	tablespoon fresh parsley sprigs
2	teaspoons strongly flavored prepared mustard
1/2	teaspoon salt
1/2	teaspoon pepper

Process all ingredients in blender until creamy, about 2 minutes. Refrigerate, covered, until ready to use.

HERBED YOGURT DRESSING
MAKES ABOUT 1 CUP.

1	container (8 fluid ounces) plain lowfat yogurt
2	tablespoons dried chives
1	tablespoon cider vinegar
1	tablespoon dried parsley

        1   teaspoon prepared mustard
    ⅛   teaspoon salt
    ⅛   teaspoon pepper

Process all ingredients in blender on low speed until well mixed, 10 to 15 seconds. Refrigerate, covered, until ready to use. Serve with mixed green salads.

BUTTERMILK DRESSING
MAKES ABOUT 1½ CUPS.

    1½   cups buttermilk
    1¼   tablespoons frozen apple juice concentrate
        1   tablespoon fresh lemon juice
    ½   teaspoon dried minced or fresh grated onion
    ½   teaspoon dill weed or chopped fresh dill
    ¼   teaspoon pepper

In jar with tight-fitting lid, shake all ingredients until well blended. Refrigerate, covered, until ready to use.

TANGY HAWAIIAN DRESSING
MAKES ABOUT ¾ CUP.

        3   tablespoons red wine vinegar
        3   tablespoons fresh lemon juice
        3   tablespoons water
        2   tablespoons pineapple juice
        2   tablespoons grapefruit juice
        1   tablespoon tomato paste
            Artificial sweetener equivalent to 1 teaspoon sugar
    ½   teaspoon paprika
    ¼   teaspoon Worcestershire sauce
    ¼   teaspoon celery seed
    ¼   teaspoon Italian Seasoning (page 24)
    ⅛   teaspoon garlic powder or ¼ teaspoon grated garlic
        1   tablespoon chopped parsley

In jar with tight-fitting lid, shake all ingredients until well blended. Chill several hours to blend flavors.

ROQUEFORT CHEESE DRESSING
MAKES ABOUT ¾ CUP.

> ¾ cup buttermilk or plain lowfat yogurt
> 2 tablespoons shredded Roquefort cheese
> 1 tablespoon fresh lemon juice
> ¼ garlic clove, pressed through garlic press
> ⅛ teaspoon salt

Combine ingredients in small bowl. Refrigerate, covered, until ready to use.

ZERO DRESSING
MAKES ABOUT ¼ CUP.

> 2 tablespoons red wine vinegar
> 2 tablespoons tomato purée
> 2 tablespoons Italian Seasoning (page 24)
> ½ teaspoon Worcestershire sauce
>   Dash ground cinnamon
>   Dash dry mustard

Combine all ingredients.

ITALIAN DRESSING
MAKES ABOUT ¾ CUP.

> 10 ounces beef stock
> 3 tablespoons chili sauce
> 2 tablespoons vinegar
> ¼ cup grated onion

Shake ingredients in jar with tight-fitting lid until well combined.

CATSUP-YOGURT DRESSING (COCKTAIL SAUCE)
MAKES ABOUT 1¼ CUPS.

> 1 cup plain lowfat yogurt
> ¼ cup catsup
> ½ teaspoon prepared horseradish
> ¼ teaspoon Worcestershire sauce
> ¼ teaspoon salt

Pepper to taste
1/4 teaspoon chives
1/8 teaspoon dried oregano
1/8 teaspoon dried rosemary

Combine all ingredients in small bowl and blend well. Chill, covered, before serving. Refrigerate up to 1 week.

VINAIGRETTE DRESSING
MAKES ABOUT 3/4 CUP.

1/2 cup vinegar
1/4 cup cold water
Artificial sweetener to taste
1/8 teaspoon dry mustard
1/8 teaspoon garlic powder
Pinch of pepper

Shake water with vinegar in jar with tight-fitting lid until blended. Add remaining ingriedents. Shake well.

YOGURT DRESSING # 1
MAKES ABOUT 1 CUP.

1 cup plain lowfat yogurt
1/2 package salad seasoning

Mix yogurt and seasoning in small bowl. Refrigerate, covered, until ready to serve.

YOGURT DRESSING # 2
MAKES ABOUT 1 1/4 CUPS.

1 cup plain lowfat yogurt
1/2 cup Lite Way Chicken Stock (page 26)
Juice of 1 medium lemon
1 teaspoon Dijon-style mustard
Salt and pepper to taste

Combine all ingredients in small bowl. Refrigerate, covered, until ready to use.

VEGETABLES

Do you think you hate vegetables? You probably turned your nose up at overcooked vegetables as a child and grew up without discovering how good they taste or the many easy ways they can be cooked. Lite Way recipes will teach you new ways of cooking vegetables that will make you regret all the times you said, "Vegetables? Ugh!"

But first, forget frying and all those rich sauces—too many calories:

	Calories
Eggplant (1 cup)	
steamed..............................	40
fried..................................	80
Parmesan	480
Cabbage (1 cup)	
steamed..............................	0–10
red canned............................	100
cole slaw	120
coleslaw/diet mayonnaise.................	40
2 rolls of stuffed cabbage	260
Onions (1 cup)	
steamed..............................	32
creamed..............................	120
french fried	170
Green Beans (Italian, French, and whole) (½ cup)	
steamed..............................	13–25
in butter sauce	40–51
in mushroom sauce	50–100

Lima Beans (¹/₂ cup)   Calories
  steamed............................... 90–110
  in butter 135

Corn (¹/₂ cup)
  steamed............................... 70–90
  creamed............................... 90–112

Broccoli (1 cup)
  steamed............................... 27
  with butter........................... 60
  with cheese........................... 70
  with hollandaise 100

Asparagus (1 cup)
   1 Cup Cooked
  plain................................. 10–20
  with butter........................... 60
  with hollandaise 85–100

Sweet Potato (1 cup)
  plain................................. 155
  candied 295

String Beans (1 cup)
  plain................................. 30
  stir fried............................ 70
  with bouillon, herbs, lemon 30–40
  with hollandaise 80
  with mushroom casserole.............. 140

Potatoes (¹/₂ cup)
  plain, mashed 55
  mashed with milk 100
  hash brown 175
  french fried 215
  pan fried............................. 230
  baked, 2¹/₂ inch 45

Lettuce and One Medium Tomato
  no dressing 25
  1 tablespoon French dressing.......... 90
  1 tablespoon mayonnaise 125
  1 tablespoon Lite Way mayonnaise...... 31–45

GENERAL SUGGESTIONS FOR LITE VEGETABLES

1. Steam rather than boil vegetables to lose less flavor.
2. Add a bay leaf to vegetables while they are steaming.
3. Boil vegetables in bouillon, white wine, and a little lemon juice, if desired, instead of water for a change.
4. Sprinkle fresh lime juice or vinegar on broccoli, brussels sprouts and green beans.
5. Broil crisp baked potato skins with a dusting of Parmesan cheese.
6. Sprinkle carrots with a little ginger or nutmeg.
7. Lightly cook chopped mushrooms with chopped onions in a little stock or bouillon; mix with cooked vegetables.
8. Top vegetables with a mixture of mustard and curry powder.
9. Splash a little soy sauce on rice.
10. Scatter fresh snipped dill, parsley, or chives on boiled potatoes; or use chives mixed with plain lowfat yogurt as a topping.
11. Serve cold cooked vegetables with vinegar or a plain lowfat yogurt dressing.
12. Sprinkle steamed or stewed vegetables with fresh herbs and spices. Avoid frying vegetables or serving them with cream or butter.

STIR FRYING

Cooking vegetables quickly in a very little oil and a bit of stock or broth until they are just crisp-tender is truly the Lite Way.

The method is easy. Cut vegetables into small equal pieces. Heat oil in nonstick pan or wok. Add vegetables to pan, stirring over medium-high heat until vegetables are coated with oil. Add stock or broth and cook, stirring, for 3 to 5 minutes, depending on the firmness of the vegetables. Check frequently to make sure the vegetables don't overcook so they retain their fresh color and taste.

Serve immediately. Sprinkle with freshly ground pepper, soy sauce, or sesame seeds.

EGGPLANT-ZUCCHINI LASAGNA
SERVES 4.

> ½   cup red wine
> 2   cups tomato juice
> 1   small diced onion
> 1   diced green pepper

  1 teaspoon dried oregano
  Salt and pepper to taste
  Artificial sweetener to equal 1 teaspoon sugar
  1 eggplant, thinly sliced
  2 large zucchini, thinly sliced lengthwise
  ½ cup grated Parmesan cheese

Filling

  2 cups lowfat cottage cheese
  2 eggs
  ½ cup chopped parsley
  ½ cup snipped fresh chives or chopped scallions

Combine wine, tomato juice, onion, green pepper, oregano, salt, pepper, and sweetener in medium saucepan. Simmer until thickened, about 1 hour. Combine cottage cheese, eggs, parsley, and chives in medium bowl. Alternate vegetables in layers with sauce and filling. Sprinkle with Parmesan cheese. Bake in 350° oven for 1 hour.

SWEET AND SOUR CABBAGE
SERVES 6.

  1 red cabbage shredded
  1 small onion chopped
  1 small apple diced
  ¾ cup water
  1 teaspoon brown sugar sweetener
  2 teaspoons fresh lemon juice

Combine all the ingredients in medium saucepan. Simmer, covered, 30 minutes, stirring several times. Serve hot or cold.

FAVORITE VEGETABLE-CHEESE BAKE

  Broccoli, cauliflower, zucchini, green beans, and/or carrots
  Skim-milk mozzarella cheese, sliced

Cut vegetables into small, uniform pieces. Steam until crisp-tender. Place vegetables in baking dish. Cover vegetables with cheese. Bake in 350° oven until cheese is bubbly and light golden, 5 to 8 minutes.

EASY EGGPLANT PARMESAN # 1
SERVES 1.

   2   slices (½ inch) peeled eggplant
   2   slices tomato
   2   ounces part-skim mozzarella cheese, sliced
       Dash dried oregano

Place eggplant slices in small baking dish. Place tomato slices over eggplant and cover with slices of cheese. Sprinkle with oregano. Bake in 350° oven until cheese is golden and eggplant soft, about 50 minutes.

EASY EGGPLANT PARMESAN # 2
SERVES 4.

   1   cup tomato juice
   1   small onion, diced
   1   clove garlic, crushed
   1   teaspoon dried oregano
   1   teaspoon dried basil
   8   slices (½ inch) eggplant
   2   tablespoons grated Parmesan cheese

Combine tomato juice, onion, garlic, oregano, and basil in small saucepan. Simmer until reduced to ½ cup. Place eggplant slices in small baking dish. Cover with 2 tablespoons tomato sauce. Sprinkle with Parmesan and bake in 350° oven for about 30 minutes.

MOCK MASHED POTATO (Mashed Cauliflower)
SERVES 4.

   1   small onion, chopped
   1   green pepper, chopped
   2   teaspoons corn oil
   2   cups diced cooked cauliflower
   ¼   teaspoon dill weed
   ¼   teaspoon dried oregano
       Salt and pepper to taste

Sauté onion and green pepper in oil in nonstick pan for 5 minutes over medium heat. Add cauliflower and toss until heated through. Add dill, oregano, and salt and pepper. Transfer to bowl and mash. Serve hot.

MOCK POTATO SALAD
SERVES 4.

> 2 cups steamed cauliflower, cut into chunks or slices
> 3 tablespoons chopped scallions
> 3 tablespoons chopped fresh parsley
> 2 tablespoons diced green pepper
> 2 hard-boiled eggs, diced
> 1/4 cup Lite Way Mayonnaise (page 178)

Combine all the ingredients in medium bowl. Chill, covered.

VEGETABLE STUFFING
MAKES 3 CUPS.

> 1 cup chopped mushrooms
> 1 cup chopped onions
> 3/4 cup Light Way Chicken Stock (page 26)
> Fresh snipped dill
> Garlic powder
> Salt and pepper
> 1 egg, beaten
> 6 cups chopped broccoli, string beans, carrots, zucchini, celery, and/or cauliflower

Cook mushrooms and onions in saucepan with chicken stock for 15 to 20 minutes. Season to taste with dill, garlic powder, and salt and pepper. Add in beaten egg. Combine with chopped vegetables. Bake 1 hour in 350° oven in separate dish, or as a veal, chicken, or turkey stuffing.

EGGPLANT "CAVIAR"
MAKES 2½ CUPS.

> 1 medium eggplant
> 2 tomatoes, peeled, chopped
> 1 small onion, grated
> 1 garlic clove, minced
> 2 tablespoons red wine vinegar
> 2 teaspoons vegetable oil
> 2 tablespoons chopped fresh parsley
> 1/2 teaspoon dried marjoram
> 1/2 teaspoon salt
> Pepper to taste

Bake eggplant in 400° oven for 1 hour. Peel and mash eggplant in medium bowl. Add other ingredients. Mix well and chill, covered.

ZUCCHINI PIZZA
MAKES 6 SERVINGS.

$\frac{1}{2}$ cup chopped onion
$\frac{3}{4}$ cup stock or bouillon
1 teaspoon salt
4 cups coarsely grated zucchini
3 eggs, lightly beaten
$\frac{1}{3}$ cup all-purpose flour
$\frac{1}{2}$ cup grated Parmesan cheese
$\frac{1}{2}$ teaspoon basil leaves, crumbled
$\frac{1}{8}$ teaspoon pepper
$\frac{1}{2}$ cup grated part-skim milk mozzarella cheese
2 tomatoes, sliced
$1\frac{1}{2}$ cups zucchini slices

Cook onion in saucepan with stock until softened, about 5 minutes; set aside. Sprinkle salt over grated zucchini on large plate. Set aside for 10 minutes; then rinse zucchini under cold water. Gently squeeze out any excess moisture from zucchini with paper towels. In large bowl beat eggs, flour, Parmesan cheese, basil, and pepper. Stir in mozzarella cheese, grated zucchini, and onion; stir until well mixed. Coat a 12-inch pizza pan with vegetable cooking spray. Spread zucchini mixture evenly over pizza pan to edges. Bake in 350° oven 25 minutes or until "pizza" is very lightly browned and dry on top. Overlap tomato slices and zucchini slices on surface of "pizza". Bake about 8 minutes more or until vegetables are just heated through.

BROCCOLI WITH MUSTARD SAUCE
MAKES 3 SERVINGS.

1 package (10 ounces) frozen broccoli spears or fresh
     broccoli
$\frac{1}{2}$ cup water
1 chicken bouillon cube or 1 tablespoon Lite Way Chicken
     Stock (p. 26)
1 tablespoon non-fat dry milk powder
2 teaspoons prepared mustard

Cook broccoli in saucepan with water and stock base until broccoli is crisp-tender. Remove broccoli with slotted spoon to serving dish. Stir milk powder and mustard into hot liquid in saucepan. Pour over broccoli.

ASPARAGUS WITH FRESH HERBS
MAKES 4 SERVINGS.

2 pounds asparagus, trimmed
10 fresh basil leaves
4 fresh mint leaves
   Juice of 2 lemons
1 small bunch fresh chives
6 sprigs flat-leaf parsley
   Coarse salt and pepper to taste
1 tablespoon olive oil

Stand asparagus, tips up, in deep saucepan in two inches of water. Steam, covered, until al dente (6-8 minutes). Remove asparagus to a serving platter. Meanwhile, make sauce. Combine basil, mint, lemon juice, chives, parsley, salt, and pepper in blender or food processor. Add olive oil. Process until smooth. Correct seasonings and pour sauce over asparagus. Serve at room temperature.

PUREED BROCCOLI
MAKES 4 SERVINGS.

   Broccoli
   Pepper to taste
   Fresh lime juice to taste

Wash broccoli well and drain. Cut off and discard tough lower parts of stalk. Divide into 3-inch long flowerets. Peel stalks. Blanch broccoli in large kettle of boiling water until a knife easily pierces the stems, about 5 minutes. Drain immediately and place in food processor. Add pepper and lime juice to taste. Purée, scraping down the sides, as necessary. Serve immediately.

MINI EGGPLANT PIZZA
MAKES 4 SERVINGS

1 Eggplant (large), tomato (large, chopped), onion (large, diced)
1 tablespoon oil
¼ cup chicken broth
2 tablespoons grated Parmesan cheese

Cook onion in ¼ cup chicken stock over medium heat for 10 minutes. Add chopped tomato and cook another 6-8 minutes. Peel and slice eggplant into ½-inch rounds. Brush lightly with oil and broil briefly to soften. Top each round with tomato-onion mix, scatter with Parmesan cheese, and broil until cheese bubbles. Cut each round into halves and serve as hors d'oeuvre.

SAVORY BEANS AND MUSHROOMS
MAKES 5 SERVINGS.

- ½ pound fresh green beans, cut into 1-inch pieces
- 1 teaspoon tarragon leaves
- ⅛ teaspoon pepper
- 1 tablespoon fresh lemon juice
- 2½ cups sliced mushrooms (about ½ pound)

Place beans in saucepan containing 1 inch boiling water, tarragon, pepper, and lemon juice. Boil, uncovered, 5 minutes. Add mushrooms and cook 5 minutes longer.

NEAPOLITAN ZUCCHINI
MAKES 4 SERVINGS.

- 1 pound zucchini, cut into ½-inch rounds
- 1 pound tomatoes, peeled, diced
- 1 teaspoon oregano leaves
- 1 teaspoon instant minced onion
- ½ teaspoon garlic powder or 1 teaspoon grated fresh garlic
- ¼ teaspoon coarsely ground black pepper

Combine squash in medium saucepan with remaining ingredients. Cook, covered, over medium heat until zucchini is tender, about 15 minutes.

SYRIAN CRUNCH
MAKES 1 SERVING.

- ¼ cup bean sprouts
- ¼ cup chopped mushrooms
- ¼ cup shredded red cabbage
- ¼ cup diced tomato
- 2 ounces skim-milk mozzarella, sliced
- 1 slice whole-wheat Syrian bread (5 inch)

Warm all the ingredients except the bread on baking sheet in 350° oven until cheese melts. Stuff ingredients into bread just before serving. Serve hot or cold.

GLAZED CARROTS
MAKES 1 SERVING.

- 1 cup (8 ounces) cooked whole baby carrots, drained
- 1 medium orange, peeled, diced
- ¼ teaspoon imitation butter flavor
- 1 tablespoon brown sugar replacement or artificial sweetener to taste
  Dash ground cinnamon

Combine all ingredients in saucepan and heat thoroughly over medium heat for 5-10 minutes.

CANDIED SQUASH
½ CUP MAKES 1 SERVING.

- 1 acorn or butternut squash, peeled, cut up into 1-inch pieces
- ½ cup water
- 2 chicken bouillon cubes
- 1 cup diet cherry soda
  Dash ground cinnamon

Peel and cut up 1 acorn or butternut squash. Cook in ½ cup water with 2 chicken bouillon cubes in covered saucepan for 5 to 10 minutes. Drain; place squash in casserole. Add diet cherry soda and cinnamon. Bake in 350° oven for 35 to 45 minutes, depending on quantity, until fork tender.

GREEK MUSHROOMS
MAKES 3 SERVINGS.

     2   cups chopped mushrooms
    ½   cup chopped green and red peppers
    ½   cup bean sprouts
    ½   cup cooked or canned bamboo shoots, drained and
             chopped
    ½   cup tomato juice
    ½   clove garlic, minced
         Salt and pepper to taste

Combine all the above ingredients.

SQUASH CREOLE
MAKES 8 SERVINGS.

    ½   cup chopped green onion
     1   cup broth
     2   pounds small squash or zucchini, cut diagonally into
             ½-inch slices
     1   teaspoon salt
         Dash pepper
     1   can (1 pound) stewed tomatoes

Cook onion in broth in large skillet until tender. Add squash, salt,
and pepper. Toss together lightly. Cook, covered, over low heat,
about 15 minutes, until squash is tender. Add stewed tomatoes
and toss. Cook, covered, 1 minute more, until heated through.

EGGPLANT CREOLE
MAKES 4 SERVINGS.

     3   cups tomato juice
     1   green pepper, coarsely diced
     2   tablespoons dehydrated onion flakes
         Salt and pepper to taste
     4   cups diced, cooked, peeled eggplant
    ½   cup water

Combine all ingredients in sauce pan except eggplant and water.
Heat to boiling; reduce heat and simmer 20-25 minutes, or until

mixture is reduced by about half, or pepper is tender. Place eggplant in baking dish. Pour sauce over eggplant. Add water and mix well. Bake in 175° oven about 15 minutes.

SAUCY GREEN BEANS
MAKES 4 SERVINGS.

- 2 packages (10 ounces each) frozen French-style green beans or 1 pound fresh green beans steamed in 1 cup water
- ½ green pepper, finely diced
- 1 tablespoon grated onion
- ½ teaspoon garlic powder or 1 teaspoon grated garlic
- 1 beef bouillon cube, crumbled (may substitute salt-free cube)
- 1 chicken bouillon cube, crumbled (may substitute salt-free cube)

Cook beans according to package directions. Remove from heat. Do not drain. Add remaining ingredients and mix. Remove 1 cup beans and liquid and place in blender. Blend until smooth. Pour over rest of beans; combine, heat, and serve.

HERBED ZUCCHINI
MAKES 6 SERVINGS.

- 6 medium zucchini (about 1½ pounds)
- ½ teaspoon salt
- 1 teaspoon mixed salad herbs (chopped fresh parsley, chives, basil, rosemary, etc.)
- ½ cup water

Trim zucchini; halve each crosswise. Make 4 or 5 cuts in each half, starting at cut end and cutting almost to tip. Combine with salt, herbs, and water in frying pan. Cook, covered, over medium heat 10 minutes or until crisp-tender; drain. Place on heated serving plates; spread cuts to form a fan.

SAVORY ZUCCHINI
MAKES 4–6 SERVINGS.

> 1/2 cup beef bouillon or broth
> 1 small onion, finely chopped
> 1 pound zucchini, thinly sliced
> 1 large tomato, peeled, coarsely chopped
> 1 small garlic clove, crushed
> 1/2 teaspoon salt
> Dash pepper
> 1 tablespoon imitation bacon bits

Cook onion in large saucepan with bouillon until tender (10-15 minutes), stirring occasionally. Stir zucchini, tomato, garlic, salt, and pepper into onion in pan. Cover and cook 10 to 15 minutes, until zucchini is tender. Place in serving bowl and sprinkle with imitation bacon bits.

MASHED TURNIPS
MAKES 4 SERVINGS.

> 1 pound yellow turnips, peeled, diced
> 1/4 teaspoon imitation butter flavor
> Salt and white pepper to taste

Place turnips in saucepan and cover with water. Heat to boiling and cook until tender, 10 to 15 minutes. Drain. Add remaining ingredients and whip until light and fluffy.

CAPONATA
MAKES 4 SERVINGS.

> 3/4 cup diced onion
> 1/2 cup green pepper, cut into 1/2-inch dice
> 1 1/2 cups diced (1/2 inch) pared eggplant
> 1 1/2 cups sliced (1/2 inch) zucchini
> 1 1/2 cups chopped canned tomatoes
> 1 cup tomato purée
> 1 packet instant chicken broth or 1 cup chicken stock
> 1 teaspoon dried basil
> 1/2 teaspoon dried oregano
> 1/8 teaspoon garlic powder

    1   cup red wine vinegar
    2   teaspoons capers, drained
        Dash artificial sweetener
        Salt and pepper to taste

In medium saucepan, combine onion and green pepper. Add water to cover. Heat to boiling; lower heat and simmer until green pepper is tender (3-5 minutes). Drain; set aside. In medium pan, combine eggplant and zucchini. Add water to cover. Heat to boiling; lower heat and simmer until eggplant is tender. Drain; set aside. In pan, combine chopped tomatoes, purée, broth mix, basil, oregano, and garlic powder. Heat to boiling; lower heat and simmer 1 hour. Add cooked vegetables, vinegar, capers, sweetener, salt, and pepper. Mix well. Chill.

ZUCCHINI à la TOMATO
MAKES 6 SERVINGS.

    2   pounds zucchini, cut into 1-inch slices
    1   can (15 ounces) tomato sauce with tomato bits
    2   cups water
    2   tablespoons grated onion
        Dash dried oregano, garlic powder, dried marjoram, and
            other spices

Combine zucchini, tomato sauce, water, onions, and spices in saucepan. Simmer 15-20 minutes.

TOMATOES ROCKEFELLER
MAKES 6 SERVINGS.

    3   large ripe tomatoes, halved
   3/4 cup chopped, drained, cooked spinach
    2   tablespoons finely chopped onion
    2   tablespoons finely chopped fresh parsley
        Dash garlic powder
        Dash pepper
        Dash paprika

Place tomatoes in shallow baking pan, cut side up. Mix spinach, onion, parsley, garlic powder, pepper, and paprika in small bowl. Spread spinach mixture over tomatoes, dividing evenly. Bake in 375° oven for 15 minutes.

BROILED MUSHROOMS

Mushrooms
Fresh lemon juice

Brush raw mushrooms with lemon juice. Broil, turning to brown all over, 5-8 minutes.

STUFFED MUSHROOM CAPS
MAKES 4 SERVINGS.

16 large fresh mushrooms, wiped clean
1/2 cup chopped fresh parsley
    Mushroom stems, drained, chopped fine
1/4 cup water
1 tablespoon soy sauce
2 tablespoons chopped scallion (head and stem)
1/4 teaspoon dried thyme
1/4 cup chicken stock or 2 packets instant chicken broth or 2 chicken bouillon cubes, crumbled (omit water if using stock)
    Pepper

Remove stems from mushrooms; reserve stems. Finely chop stems and add to remaining ingredients. Cook mixture in non-stick skillet until tender. Stuff mixture into caps. Place on baking sheet and bake in 375° oven for about 20 minutes until piping hot.

TARRAGON MUSHROOMS
MAKES 5 SERVINGS.

1 tablespoon grated Parmesan cheese
1 1/2 tablespoons snipped fresh chives
1 tablespoon chopped fresh parsley
2 teaspoons diet margarine
2 teaspoons sherry extract or 1/3 cup sherry
1 teaspoon prepared spicy mustard
1/2 teaspoon tarragon
    Salt and pepper to taste
2 cups fresh mushroom caps, wiped clean

Combine all the ingredients except mushroom caps in small bowl. Mash well. Fill mushroom caps with the stuffing, dividing evenly.

STIR FRY VEGETABLES
MAKES 8 SERVINGS.

    2   cups (½ pound) thinly sliced carrot (sliced on diagonal)
    1   cup (¼ pound) thinly sliced celery (sliced on diagonal)
    ¾   cup bouillon or stock
    ½   pound fresh snow peas, trimmed
    ¼   pound mushrooms, wiped clean, sliced lengthwise through
            stems
    2   tablespoons fresh lemon juice
    ½   teaspoon salt
        Dash pepper
    2   tablespoons chopped fresh parsley

Spray large skillet or wok with vegetable cooking spray. Heat skillet. Add carrot and celery; stir-fry for 2 minutes. Add bouillon. Stir in snow peas and mushrooms; stir-fry 2 more minutes. Cover and cook 2 minutes or until vegetables are tender. Add lemon juice, salt, and pepper. Stir. To serve, sprinkle with parsley.

BAKED TOMATO HALVES
MAKES 6 SERVINGS.

    3   large tomatoes, halved
    3   tablespoons Italian Seasoning (page 24)
    3   tablespoons grated Parmesan cheese

Place tomatoes cut side up in baking dish. Sprinkle each with ½ tablespoon Italian Seasoning and ½ tablespoon Parmesan cheese. Bake in 400° oven for 20 to 25 minutes, or until tomatoes are soft but firm.

MARINATED MUSHROOMS
MAKES 4 SERVINGS.

    ¾   cup red wine vinegar
    ½   cup water
    ½   teaspoon salt
    ½   teaspoon dried oregano
    5   peppercorns, crushed
    2   whole cloves
    1   bay leaf
    1   garlic clove, crushed
    12 large mushrooms (¾ pound)

Combine all ingredients except mushrooms in a saucepan. Heat to boiling; cook 1 or 2 minutes. Add mushrooms. Cover. Lower heat; simmer 5 minutes. Allow mushrooms to cool in liquid, at room temperature. Transfer to glass or plastic container; cover and chill 2 to 3 days.

MUSTARD BEETS
MAKES 4 SERVINGS.

    1   can (10 ounces) sliced beets, drained
    ⅓   cup thinly sliced red onions
    ½   cup plain lowfat yogurt
    1   tablespoon prepared mustard
    2   teaspoons white vinegar
    4   whole cloves
        Salt and pepper to taste

Combine beets and onions in bowl. In separate bowl, combine remaining ingredients; pour over beets and onions. Toss to blend. Remove cloves just before serving.

BROCCOLI VINAIGRETTE
MAKES 2 SERVINGS.

    1   package (10 ounces) frozen broccoli spears, or ½ bunch
            fresh broccoli blanched or steamed crisply (about 1
            pound)
    ½   cup wine vinegar
    2   tablespoons cold water
    1   tablespoon salad oil
    2   teaspoons grated onion
    1   teaspoon finely snipped fresh chives
    1   teaspoon chopped queen-size green olives
    ½   teaspoon chopped fresh parsley
    ½   teaspoon paprika
    ½   teaspoon salt
    ⅛   teaspoon pepper

Cook broccoli according to package directions. Drain well. Combine vinegar, water, oil, onion, chives, olives, parsley, paprika, salt, and pepper in jar with tight-fitting lid. Shake jar until thoroughly blended. Arrange broccoli on serving platter. Pour sauce over. Chill, covered, until serving time.

RATATOUILLE #1

MAKES 6-8 SERVINGS.

1	large eggplant, peeled and diced (2 cups)
2	medium zucchini, sliced into ½-inch rounds (2 cups)
1½	cups broth
1½	cups coarsely chopped onion
2	green peppers, cut into squares
3	tomatoes, chopped (1 cup)
3	tablespoons minced fresh parsley
2	garlic cloves, minced
½	teaspoon oregano
½	teaspoon basil
⅛	teaspoon pepper
5	tablespoons tomato paste

Cook eggplant and zucchini over low heat in 1 cup broth in Dutch oven for about 15 minutes. Remove and set aside. Cook onion, garlic, and green peppers in remaining ½ cup broth until tender, about 10 minutes. Add tomatoes, parsley, eggplant and zucchini. Sprinkle with seasonings and add tomato paste. Simmer, covered, until vegetables are tender and most of liquid has disappeared, about 30 minutes. If there is too much liquid, uncover and continue cooking until sauce thickens. Serve hot or cold.

RATATOUILLE #2

MAKES 4 SERVINGS (½ CUP PER SERVING).

2	cups cubed (1 inch) eggplant
2	cups cubed (1 inch) zucchini
2	medium green peppers cut into 1-inch square pieces
2	medium tomatoes, cut into 1-inch square pieces
2	cups tomato juice
¼	cup chopped fresh parsley
2	tablespoons dehydrated onion flakes
1	teaspoon dried marjoram or oregano
2	garlic cloves, lightly crushed
	Salt and pepper to taste

Combine all ingredients in large saucepan. Heat to boiling; lower heat and cook covered until vegetables are tender, stirring frequently to prevent scorching, about 30 minutes. If there is too much liquid, uncover and continue cooking until sauce thickens. Serve hot or cold.

For a quick lunch add 2 ounces part-skim mozzarella cheese, grated, to 1 cup ratatouille. Bake for 20 minutes at 350°.

PIZZA IN A HURRY
MAKES 1 SERVING.

> 1 slice toasted rye bread or ½ whole wheat 7-inch pita (split horizontally)
> 4 tablespoons tomato juice
> 2 ounces part-skim mozzarella cheese, grated
> Dash dried oregano and garlic powder

Place cheese on toast or pita. Spread tomato juice over cheese; sprinkle with oregano and garlic powder. Broil until melted.

POULTRY, FISH, AND MEAT

The meat-and-potato eaters of days past have learned a lesson: too much fat, too much cholesterol, too many calories. They now eat poultry and fish, and what's more, they love it! When they do stray, they prepare new cuts of meat in new ways of cooking that make the old heavily marbled sirloin steak look barbarian.

Using Lite Way recipes will give you the taste and the excitement that comes from a healthy as well as a hit meal. You won't go back to the old way, and here is the reason:

The Lite Way	Calories	The old way	Calories
Roasted chicken	160	Fried chicken	232
Stewed chicken	150	Creamed chicken	416
Leftover cooked turkey	176	Turkey pot pie	442
Poached sole	100	Sole almondine	450
Flounder in fresh lemon juice	100	Fried flounder	350

The Lite Way dresses up your entrée in such tasty trappings that you will wish you have used it for years.

GENERAL SUGGESTIONS FOR POULTRY, FISH AND MEAT

1. Buy broiler-fryer chickens—they are less fatty than roasters or stewing hens.
2. Young chickens and turkeys are less fatty than older ones; cornish hens are very low in fat.

3. Light meat is less fatty than dark.

4. Avoid duck and goose—they have three times the fat content of other fowl.

5. Removing the skin from poultry before cooking can eliminate 25% of the fat.

6. Trim away all poultry fat before or after cooking.

7. Since you cannot roast a turkey without skin, puncture the skin before roasting so the fat will run off.

8. Do not make gravy from pan drippings until you have refrigerated them and skimmed off the fat.

9. Do not buy a self-basting turkey—it is injected with butter and oil.

10. Baste with bouillon spiced with your favorite seasonings, wine, or marinade.

11. Do not eat the skin of fish—it is fatty.

12. Trim away the fat from fish before cooking.

13. Poach or broil fish in fresh lemon juice. Do not fry or broil in butter.

14. When buying fresh fish you may have to buy a larger piece (or a whole fish) than you need for a meal. Cook all the fish and save the remainder for a fish salad.

15. Lean beef, with no marblization and as little visible fat as possible, and veal are the best meats for Lite Way cooking.

16. Tenderize lean meat by marinating, braising in bouillon, Lite Way stock, or pounding with heavy clean skillet.

17. Before cooking, trim off all fat from meat.

18. You can reduce the fattiness of meat by broiling or grilling—the fat drips off.

19. Many of your favorite veal recipes can be made with chicken instead with little change of flavor, texture, or appearance.

20. Slow cooking renders more fat than high heat.

21. Reduce or cook down sauces for better flavor.

22. Watch your kinds of meat:

1 pound	Beef	Veal	Lamb	Pork
rib steak or chop	875 calories	709 calories	612 calories	857 calories

23. Without the fat of its grownup counterpart, veal is an excellent Lite Way choice:

3½ ounces		
	Veal rib chops	210
	Beef rib steaks	450

Poultry

QUICK AND EASY CHICKEN 'N VEGETABLES
MAKES 1 SERVING.

> 4 ounces leftover chicken or whole boned chicken breast
> 1 package (10 ounces) frozen vegetables, such as broccoli or Chinese vegetables
> ½ cup chicken bouillon
> 1 tablespoon soy sauce
> Garlic powder to taste

Coat nonstick skillet with vegetable cooking spray. Cook chicken over medium heat 15-20 minutes. Add vegetables, bouillon, soy sauce, and garlic powder. Serve as soon as vegetables are heated through.

CHICKEN À L'ORANGE
MAKES 4 SERVINGS.

> 3 pounds frying chicken pieces, trimmed of fat
> ½ cup orange juice
> ¼ cup fresh lemon juice
> 1 teaspoon grated lemon or orange peel (zest)
> ¼ teaspoon dried tarragon
> ¼ teaspoon dried thyme
> 2 teaspoons paprika
> 1 teaspoon garlic powder
> Salt and pepper to taste

Bake chicken pieces in a single layer in baking pan in 400° oven for 25 minutes, until skin is crisp. Pour off fat. Remove skin. Combine juices, zest, tarragon, and thyme in small bowl; pour over chicken. Sprinkle with paprika, garlic powder, and salt and pepper to taste. Bake, basting until chicken is tender, about 45 minutes. Spoon sauce over chicken to serve.

COQ AU VIN FOR ONE
MAKES 1 SERVING.

- 1 chicken breast, boned and skinned
- 3 tablespoons red wine
- 3 small pearl onions
- 3 large mushrooms

Brown chicken breast for 5 minutes over medium heat in non-stick skillet with no fat added. Pour off fat. Add red wine, onions, and mushrooms. Cover and simmer until tender, about 30 minutes. Uncover and simmer until liquid evaporates.

CHICKEN NAPOLEAN
MAKES 2 SERVINGS.

- 10 ounces boned, skinned chicken breasts
- 1/4 teaspoon garlic powder
- 1/4 teaspoon paprika
- 1/4 teaspoon dried rosemary leaves, crumbled
  Salt and pepper to taste
- 1 cup mushrooms, quartered
- 1/4 cup red wine vinegar
- 2 tablespoons chopped fresh parsley

Season chicken with garlic powder, paprika, rosemary, salt, and pepper. Broil chicken until brown on both sides; place in casserole. Cover with mushrooms, and sprinkle with vinegar and parsley. Bake covered in 350° oven until chicken is tender, about 15 minutes.

LITE WAY FRIED CHICKEN (OR VEAL) AND VARIATIONS
MAKES 1 SERVING.

- 1/4 pound chicken cutlets, or veal cutlets
- 1 tablespoon grated cheese, such as Parmesan, Romano, or American
- 1 tablespoon plain or seasoned bread crumbs

Moisten the cutlets with water. Press cutlets into the cheese, coating both sides evenly, then into the breadcrumbs. Spray a nonstick skillet with vegetable cooking spray. Arrange the coated cutlets in a single layer without touching in pan. Sauté over low-moderate heat 4 to 5 minutes until the underside is crisp and golden. Turn with spatula and cook another 4 minutes.

CHICKEN SCALLOPINI

Coat chicken cutlets with 1 tablespoon grated Parmesan cheese and 1 tablespoon Italian seasoning (see p. 00) and sauté as above. Remove cutlets to serving platter. Put 2 tablespoons dry sherry wine in skillet for each cutlet. Turn heat to high; cook, stirring, 1 to 2 minutes, until slightly reduced. Pour sauce over chicken. Garnish with chopped fresh parsley.

CHICKEN PARMIGIANA

Prepare chicken cutlets as above. Sprinkle with ½ ounce shredded or thinly sliced part-skim mozzarella. Allow cheese to melt. Remove cutlets to serving platter. Pour ¾ cup tomato juice in skillet for each serving. Add pinch of dried oregano or basil. Turn heat to high. Cook, stirring, 2 to 3 minutes until tomato juice is reduced to smooth sauce. Pour over chicken and serve.

CHICKEN PICCATA

Prepare chicken cutlets as above, using grated Romano cheese and seasoned crumbs and sauté as above. When cooked, remove chicken to a serving platter. In the skillet, combine 2 tablespoons fresh lemon juice, ¼ cup defatted chicken broth, and 1 tablespoon minced fresh parsley. Cook and stir over high heat 2 minutes until slightly reduced; pour over chicken. Garnish with lemon slices.

CHICKEN WITH MUSHROOMS

Prepare chicken cutlets as above using grated Parmesan cheese and plain bread crumbs seasoned with a pinch of nutmeg, onion powder, and pepper, and sauté as above. When cooked, remove chicken to serving platter. For each serving, put ½ cup thinly sliced mushrooms and 2 tablespoons dry sherry wine in the skillet. Turn heat to high. Cook and stir until wine and mushroom liquid evaporate and mushrooms begin to brown. Spoon hot mushrooms over chicken.

BUTTERMILK CHICKEN
MAKES 4 SERVINGS.

3	pounds chicken parts, skinned
1	tablespoon unsaturated oil
½	cup sliced scallions
2	cups drained canned whole tomatoes
¾	cup buttermilk
1	teaspoon dill weed
½	teaspoon granulated sugar
½	teaspoon salt
⅛	teaspoon pepper
	Dash Tabasco
½	cup plain lowfat yogurt
¼	cup chopped fresh parsley

Broil chicken parts on a rack in broiling pan until lightly browned on both sides; set aside. Heat oil in large nonstick skillet, add ¼ cup of the scallions and sauté until tender. In a blender container, combine next 7 ingredients and process until smooth. Add blender sauce and chicken to scallions in skillet; bring to boil. Reduce heat and simmer, covered, 20 minutes or until chicken is tender. Stir in yogurt; heat but do not boil. Remove to serving platter. Garnish with remaining ¼ cup scallions and parsley.

CHICKEN KEBABS
MAKES 4 SERVINGS.

2	whole chicken breasts, skinned, boned
1	tablespoon plain lowfat yogurt
½	teaspoon curry powder
¼	teaspoon turmeric
⅛	teaspoon dry mustard
⅛	teaspoon ground cardamom
1	teaspoon fresh lime juice
1	teaspoon vinegar
8	thin slices of onion
4	small tomatoes, halved

Cut each chicken breast into 16 squares. Combine with the yogurt, curry powder, turmeric, mustard, cardamon, lime juice, and vinegar in medium bowl and let stand ½ hour. Thread onto skewers 2 chicken pieces, onion slice, 2 chicken pieces, and tomato half. Repeat until all ingredients are used. Broil slowly, turning, basting occasionally with marinade, about 10 minutes.

CHICKEN HONOLULU
MAKES 4 SERVINGS.

> 1 chicken bouillon cube plus ½ cup boiling water or ½ cup Lite Way Chicken Stock (page 26)
> ¼ cup fresh lemon juice
> 3 tablespoons soy sauce
> 2 tablespoons grated onion
> 1 teaspoon garlic powder or 1 tablespoon fresh chopped garlic
> ½ teaspoon ground ginger, or 2 teaspoons fresh chopped ginger
> ¼ teaspoon pepper
> chicken (about 2½ pounds) quartered, trimmed of fat

Use Lite Way stock or dissolve bouillon cube in boiling water. Add lemon juice, soy sauce, onion, garlic, ginger, and pepper; mix well. Pour over chicken in large bowl, turning well to coat all sides. Cover and refrigerate 3 to 4 hours, turning once. Arrange chicken pieces on rack in broiler pan. Place under a preheated moderate broiler until chicken is fork tender, about 45 minutes, turning and brushing frequently with marinade.

CHICKEN PAPRIKASH
MAKES 2 SERVINGS.

> 1¼ pounds skinned, boned chicken, trimmed of fat
> ½ cup onion, finely diced
> 1 medium green pepper, diced
> 2 cups chicken bouillon or Lite Way Chicken Stock (page 26)
> 1 tablespoon paprika
> 1 cup buttermilk

Layer the chicken in a 1½ quart baking dish. Brown onion and pepper in heated nonstick skillet sprayed with vegetable cooking spray at moderately high heat for about 5 minutes, stirring to prevent scorching. Add chicken bouillon and paprika and heat to boiling; pour over chicken in baking dish. Cover and bake in 375° oven for 1 hour or until chicken is tender. Ten minutes before serving, add buttermilk to dish. Mix well and bake 10 minutes more or until buttermilk is heated through. Serve chicken with sauce well mixed.

LIME BAKED CHICKEN
MAKES 6 SERVINGS.

	Juice of 1 lime
	Juice of 1 lime
1	tablespoon oil
1	clove garlic, crushed
	Salt and pepper to taste
1/2	teaspoon curry powder
1/4	teaspoon ground ginger
6	chicken thighs, skinned

Line shallow pan with foil; grease lightly. Combine all the ingredients except the chicken in a small bowl; coat chicken with mixture. Arrange chicken, bone down, in baking pan. Bake in 400° oven about 55 minutes or until tender.

CHICKEN WITH EGGPLANT
MAKES 4 SERVINGS.

2 1/2	pounds skinned chicken, trimmed of fat
1	clove garlic, lightly crushed
2	cups peeled eggplant, cut into 3-by-1/2-inch pieces
2	cups diced mushrooms (1/4 pound)
2	medium tomatoes, quartered
2	medium green peppers, cut into squares
8	ounces small onions, parboiled in water to cover for 10 minutes
3/4	cup chicken bouillon or Lite Way Chicken Stock (page 26)
1	bay leaf
1	teaspoon mixed dried herbs including basil and thyme

Rub chicken with garlic. Put chicken in a 2 1/2 quart casserole. Combine vegetables and remaining ingredients and spread over chicken. Cover and bake in 375° oven for 40 to 50 minutes or until chicken is tender. To evaporate excess liquid, continue baking without cover. Mix well before serving.

DILLED CHICKEN
MAKES 4 SERVINGS.

1	broiler-fryer chicken (about 2½ pounds) quartered, trimmed of fat
3	tablespoons grated garlic
2	teaspoons pepper
1	tablespoon diet margarine
¼	teaspoon dill weed or 1 teaspoon fresh dill
¼	cup fresh lime juice

Sprinkle chicken with grated garlic and pepper. Grease 2½ quart baking dish with part of margarine. Place chicken in dish and dot with remaining margarine. Sprinkle with dill weed and lime juice. Bake, covered, in 450° oven 45 minutes or until chicken is tender.

GREEK BAKED CHICKEN WITH LEMON
MAKES 4 SERVINGS.

	Chicken (about 2½ pounds), skinned, cut up, trimmed of fat
½	lemon
¼	teaspoon paprika
⅛	teaspoon pepper
¼	cup chicken bouillon or Lite Way Chicken Stock (page 26)
1	lemon, sliced

Rub chicken pieces on all sides with cut lemon. Sprinkle with paprika and pepper. Bake in shallow pan at 350° for 15 minutes. Pour in bouillon. Bake 45 minutes more, until chicken is tender, turning several times. Put lemon slices on top of chicken. Serve hot.

LEMON 'N GARLIC BAKED CHICKEN
MAKES 4 SERVINGS.

    Broiler-fryer chicken (2-2½ pound), quartered, skinned, trimmed of fat
1 large clove garlic, crushed
2 teaspoons dried rosemary leaves
½ teaspoon salt
    Dash pepper
1 teaspoon grated lemon zest
⅓ cup fresh lemon juice
½ cup water

Place chicken in shallow 2½ quart baking dish. Combine garlic, rosemary, salt, pepper, and lemon zest in small bowl. Sprinkle over chicken. Pour lemon juice and water over all. Bake, uncovered, in 400° oven for 30 minutes. Turn chicken. Baste with pan liquids. Continue baking another 25 to 30 minutes until chicken is tender.

SAVORY BROILED CHICKEN
MAKES 4 SERVINGS.

1 tablespoon pickling spice
1 teaspoon curry powder
¾ teaspoon poultry seasoning
½ teaspoon salt
1 cup beef bouillon or Lite Way Beef Stock (page 26)
2 tablespoons fresh lemon juice
4 half chicken breasts (about 5 ounces each)

Combine pickling spice, curry, poultry seasoning, salt, bouillon, and lemon juice in small saucepan. Warm over low heat; do not boil. Pour over chicken in bowl. Cover and refrigerate 24 hours, turning chicken several times. Broil chicken 4 inches from heat for 20 minutes until tender, turning chicken during broiling and basting several times.

HAWAIIAN CHICKEN
MAKES 6 SERVINGS.

  1 can (13¾ ounces) chicken broth, undiluted, or 2 cups Lite
      Way Chicken Stock (page 26)
  1 pound chicken breasts, skinned, sliced
  ½ cup julienned bamboo shoots (about 4 ounces)
  1 can (8 ounces) water chestnuts, drained, sliced
  3 stalks celery, julienned
  ¼ pound mushrooms, washed, sliced (2 cups)
  1 large yellow onion, peeled, sliced
  1 slice (¼ inch thick) gingerroot or 2 teaspoons red ginger,
      blotted, julienned*
2 to 3 tablespoons oyster sauce
  ½ teaspoon salt
  1 can (8 ounces) pineapple chunks, in unsweetened juice,
      drained (reserve liquid)
  ¼ pound fresh spinach, washed, trimmed, chopped into
      bite-size pieces
  ¼ cup thinly sliced red pepper

Heat large heavy skillet or wok over medium heat until hot. Add ½
cup broth to pan coated with vegetable cooking spray. Add sliced
chicken and stir fry about 2 minutes. Add bamboo shoots, water
chestnuts, celery, mushrooms, onion, gingerroot, oyster sauce,
and salt; stir fry a few more minutes or just until chicken is no
longer pink. Add 1 cup chicken broth; cover and steam for 1
minute over high heat. Drain off excess liquid, and combine it
with reserved pineapple juice. Add pineapple chunks and spinach; mix well. Serve garnished with red pepper strips. Spoon
reserved liquid over chicken if needed.

* Red ginger slices are bottled in syrup, and can be purchased in oriental grocery
stores.

LEMON CHICKEN
MAKES 4 SERVINGS.

   1 broiler-fryer chicken (about 2½ pounds) cut up, trimmed of
       fat
   1 medium onion, minced (½ cup)
   3 tablespoons fresh lemon juice
   2 tablespoons soy sauce
  ½ teaspoon dried leaf tarragon, crumbled
  ¼ teaspoon paprika
  ¼ teaspoon salt
  ⅛ teaspoon pepper
     Fresh parsley
     Lemon slices

Place chicken in a 2½ quart shallow non-stick roasting pan, skin side up. Bake, uncovered, in 450° oven for 20 minutes to melt fat and crisp the skin. Drain off fat; remove skin. Combine remaining ingredients in small bowl; pour on chicken and turn to coat. Bake, uncovered, in 175° oven for 30 more minutes or until chicken is tender, basting once. Garnish with parsley and lemon slices.

CHICKEN CACCIATORE
MAKES 4 SERVINGS.

   1 broiler-fryer chicken (about 2 pounds), cut up, trimmed of
       fat
   1 can (1 pound) whole tomatoes
   1 small green pepper, chopped (½ cup)
   1 medium onion, chopped (½ cup)
   1 teaspoon fresh grated garlic
  ½ teaspoon Italian Seasoning (page 24) or dried leaf oregano,
       crumbled

Place chicken, skin side up, in 2½ quart baking dish. Bake, uncovered, in 450° oven for 20 minutes. Remove from oven, drain fat; remove skin. Combine remaining ingredients in small bowl and pour over chicken. Bake, uncovered, in 350° oven for 40 more minutes, basting frequently, or until chicken is tender.

CHICKEN PARMIGIANA
MAKES 1 SERVING.

    2½   ounces skinned, boned chicken breast
         Salt and pepper to taste
    ½   cup chicken bouillon
    1   ounce part-skim mozzarella cheese, sliced

Season chicken with salt and pepper. Broil in shallow pan 4 inches from heat, basting frequently with bouillon; turn once. Top chicken with slice of mozzarella cheese and bake in 400° oven for 8 to 10 minutes, until cheese melts and browns slightly.

CHICKEN SUKIYAKI
MAKES 2 SERVINGS.

    1   clove garlic, minced
    ½   cup Lite Way Chicken Stock (page 26)
    1   cup thinly sliced celery
    1   cup thinly sliced asparagus
    ½   cup minced green pepper
    1   cup thinly sliced mushrooms
    1   cup diced, poached white meat chicken
    2   tablespoons soy sauce
    2   teaspoons steak sauce

Add garlic to stock in medium saucepan; bring to boil. Add vegetables and simmer 5 minutes. Stir in chicken, soy sauce, and steak sauce. Cook until heated through.

CHICKEN STIR-FRY
MAKES 4 SERVINGS.

- ½ cup chicken bouillon or Lite Way Chicken Stock (page 000)
- 1 clove garlic, minced
- 1¼ pounds chicken thigh meat (skinned, boned, poached until almost done, cut into 1-inch pieces)
- 1 ripe tomato, chunked
- 1 bunch scallions, coarsely chopped (1½ cups)
- 1 cup sliced mushrooms
- 1 cup diagonally-sliced celery
- 1 can (4 ounce) water chestnuts, drained, sliced
  Grated fresh pared gingerroot
- 2 teaspoons soy sauce
- 2 cups finely shredded iceburg lettuce

Heat broth in nonstick pan. Cook garlic 3 minutes on high heat. Reduce heat and add chicken, tomato, scallions, mushrooms, celery, water chestnuts, and ginger. Stir well; add soy sauce; stir again. Cover and simmer 5 minutes. Just before serving, toss lightly with lettuce.

CRISP MUSTARD CHICKEN
MAKES 4 SERVINGS.

- 1 roasting chicken (about 2½ pounds), trimmed of fat
- 3 tablespoons Dijon-style mustard
- 2 tablespoons fresh bread crumbs
- 1 tablespoon grated Parmesan cheese
- 1 tablespoon fresh tarragon

Place chicken, breast side down, on rack on broiling pan filled with 1-inch water. Steam covered for 30 minutes in 350° oven. Remove from oven. When chicken has cooled enough to handle, remove skin. Paint chicken with mustard. Mix bread crumbs, cheese, and tarragon in small bowl; press onto warm bird. Bake 45 minutes or until chicken is tender.

BARBECUED CHICKEN
MAKES 2 SERVINGS.

1½ cups tomato juice
¾ cup vinegar
4½ teaspoons Worcestershire sauce
2 teaspoons salt
¼ teaspoon pepper
¼ teaspoon cayenne pepper
¼ teaspoon dry mustard
1 bay leaf
   Artificial sweetener to taste
3 cloves garlic, minced
1¼ pounds skinned chicken pieces
1 cup onion, thinly sliced

Combine all ingredients except chicken and onions in medium saucepan. Simmer 15 to 20 minutes; set aside. Arrange chicken in single layer in shallow 2½ quart baking dish, cover with onion slices and sauce. Bake, uncovered, in 425° oven, basting frequently and turning once, until chicken is tender, about 25 minutes on each side.

CHICKEN CURRY WITH TOMATOES
MAKES 4 SERVINGS.

1 cup onions, diced
1 cup chicken bouillon, or Lite Way Chicken Stock (page 26)
2 tablespoons curry powder
1 cup tomato purée
1¼ pounds boned, skinned chicken breasts, diced
¾ cup hot water

Place onions, bouillon, and curry powder in casserole or skillet with lid and cook, covered, 10 to 15 minutes. Add tomato purée and stir. Add chicken. Cook, covered, stirring occasionally, until chicken is done, about 15 minutes. Add water; stir. Replace cover and cook for 5 more minutes.

INDIAN CHICKEN
MAKES 4 SERVINGS.

2½	pounds skinned chicken pieces
2	cloves garlic, mashed or pressed
1	teaspoon allspice
½	teaspoon grated fresh pared gingerroot or ¼ teaspoon ground ginger
¼	teaspoon crushed red pepper flakes
	Fresh lemon juice
1	cup buttermilk

Pierce chicken with fork. In small bowl, make paste of seasonings and enough lemon juice to moisten; rub into chicken. Bake on rack over pan in 350° oven for 45 minutes or until tender. Serve with ¼ cup heated buttermilk poured over each serving.

Fish

Lite Way Tips:

When you buy fish breaded, fried and frozen, you get only 60% fish and many, many calories.

Fish or beef:

¼ pound rib steak	450 calories
¼ pound fillet of sole	75 calories

300 + calories per pound:
clams, cod, flounder, haddock, arpters, sole, scallops

400 + calories per pound:
catfish, crabmeat, shrimp, smelts, rockfish, red snapper, perch, lobster, bass, halibut

500 + calories per pound:
bluefish, butterfish, carp, porgy, swordfish, canned tuna packed in water

700 + calories per pound:
whitefish, pompano

800 + calories per pound:
mackerel

900 + calories per pound:
salmon

1000 + calories per pound:
lake trout, canned tuna packed in oil

FLOUNDER MEXICAN
MAKES 2 SERVINGS.

1¼ pound fillet of flounder
2 small onions sliced
1 green pepper, sliced
1 8 ounce can tomato sauce
½ cup part-skim mozzarella cheese, grated

Coat nonstick baking dish with vegetable spray according to directions. Place fish in pan and cover with sliced onions, green pepper, tomato sauce, and cheese. Bake in 350° oven for 25 minutes or until fish is tender.

STUFFED RED SNAPPER
MAKES 2 SERVINGS.

1 red snapper (about 2 pounds), slit, cleaned, boned, left whole
Lite Way Vegetable Stuffing (page 69)
½ cup white wine
1 tablespoon Lemon Pepper Seasoning (page 24)
1 tablespoon fresh minced garlic

Stuff snapper with vegetable stuffing; sew to enclose stuffing. Combine wine and seasonings and pour over fish in baking pan. Bake in 350° oven for 40 minutes, basting with juices.

CHILLED POACHED SALMON
MAKES 6 SERVINGS.

2 tablespoons chopped fresh parsley
1 teaspoon tarragon vinegar or fresh lime juice
1 bay leaf
¼ teaspoon dried thyme
1 small onion, sliced
6 salmon steaks about 1 inch thick
Cucumber-Yogurt Sauce (recipe follows)

Pour water into wide skillet to depth of 1½ inches. Add all ingredients except fish and sauce to water; heat to boiling. Add fish; reduce heat and simmer until tender, 10 to 15 minutes. Chill. To serve, spoon Cucumber-Yogurt Sauce over fish.

CUCUMBER-YOGURT SAUCE
MAKES 1½ CUPS.

    1   medium cucumber, peeled, chopped fine
    1   cup plain low fat yogurt
    1   tablespoon vinegar
    1   teaspoon minced onion
    ⅛   teaspoon pepper
        Few grains cayenne

Combine all the ingredients in small bowl. Chill covered.

MARINATED SHRIMP AND ARTICHOKE
MAKES 4 SERVINGS.

Shrimp:

    3   cups dry white wine
    2   cups water
    1   large onion, thinly sliced
    1   medium carrot, peeled, thinly sliced
    1   celery stalk, thinly sliced
    6   parsley sprigs
    1   bay leaf
    6   peppercorns
    1   teaspoon fresh or ¼ teaspoon dried tarragon
    ¼   teaspoon dried thyme
    1½ pounds large raw shrimp, unpeeled

Simmer all ingredients except shrimp in kettle for 15 minutes. Bring to a rolling boil and add shrimp. Reduce heat and simmer, covered, 5 minutes. Allow shrimp to cool in the cooking liquid. Drain, peel and devein shrimp. Place in bowl and set aside.

Marinade:

    ½   cup fresh lemon juice
    2   scallions, finely sliced
    1   teaspoon finely chopped red pepper
    2   teaspoons chopped fresh parsley
    1   teaspoon dried basil
        Pepper to taste

Mix all ingredients in small bowl and pour over shrimp. Chill, covered, for 1 hour.

Artichokes:

> 4 large artichokes
>   Boiling water
> 4 coriander
>   Juice of 1 lemon
>   Tomato wedges
>   Lemon slices

Wash artichokes. Cut off tops and stems. Remove tough outside leaves. Place in a deep pot with coriander and lemon juice. Add boiling water to cover. Cook, covered, 20 to 30 minutes. Remove from water and turn upside down to drain. Chill. To serve, remove shrimp from marinade with slotted spoon and place next to artichokes on serving plate. Pour remaining sauce over artichokes. Serve cold, garnished with tomato wedges and lemon slices.

SEAFOOD CREOLE
SERVES 4.

> 1   large onion, diced (½ cup)
> 1   green pepper, diced (½ cup)
> 4   stalks celery, diced
> 1   cup tomato juice
>   Artificial sweetener to taste
> 1   teaspoon dried oregano
> 2   cups fresh bean sprouts, or 1 can, rinsed several times
> ½   cup mushrooms sliced
> 1¼   pounds cooked deveined shrimp or other fish

Simmer onion, pepper, and celery in tomato juice in medium saucepan until tender. Add sweetener and oregano. Cook 2 minutes. Add bean sprouts, mushrooms, and shrimp. Cover and simmer until shrimp are heated through, about 10 minutes.

BROILED BASS
SERVES 2.

> ¼   small onion, minced
>   Juice from ½ lemon
> ¼   cup finely chopped fresh parsley
> 9   ounces striped sea-bass fillets

Cook onion, lemon juice, and parsley in small saucepan for 3 minutes. Put fish on aluminum foil, dribble onion mixture over fish. Broil 8-10 minutes on each side, until fish easily flakes with fork.

HERBED BAKED FISH STEAK
MAKES 4 SERVINGS.

- 1½ pounds fresh halibut steak
- 1 teaspoon minced onion
- 1 teaspoon dry mustard
- ½ teaspoon oregano leaves
- ¼ teaspoon marjoram leaves
  Dash pepper
- 2 teaspoons water
- 4 teaspoons fresh lemon juice
  Paprika
  Lemon wedge (optional)

Place fish in baking dish. Combine minced onion, mustard, oregano, marjoram, and pepper with 2 teaspoons water in small bowl; let stand 10 minutes for flavors to blend. Add lemon juice. Spoon evenly over fish. Bake uncovered in a 475° oven 17 to 20 minutes or until fish flakes easily when tested with fork. Garnish with paprika, and with lemon wedge, if desired.

SCALLOP-SHRIMP BROCHETTE

Shrimp
Scallops
Fresh lime juice
Mushrooms, whole small
Green peppers, chunks
Pepper
Curry powder
Celery seed
Garlic powder

Marinate shelled shrimp and scallops in lime juice ½ hour. Alternate on skewers with mushroom and green pepper. Sprinkle pepper, curry powder, celery seed, and garlic powder over skewers. Broil or cook on grill.

TUNA HAWAIIAN STIR-FRY
MAKES 2 SERVINGS.

    1   medium green pepper, cut in strips
    1/2 cup chopped onion
    2   tablespoons chicken bouillon or Lite Way stock (page 26)
    1/2 cup orange juice
    1/4 cup cider vinegar
    1   tablespoon soy sauce
    1   teaspoon ground ginger
    1   cup pineapple, peeled, diced
    1   can (7 ounces) tuna fish packed in water, drained, cut into chunks
        Artificial sweetener to taste

Cook green peppers and onion in bouillon in medium skillet over low heat until soft; drain. Stir in orange juice, vinegar, soy sauce, and ground ginger. Cook for 1 minute or until is heated through, stirring constantly. Stir in pineapple, tuna fish, salt, and sweetener. Simmer 10 minutes until tuna fish is heated through.

TUNA RAMEKINS
MAKES 6 SERVINGS.

    2   cups fresh mushrooms, sliced
    1/4 cup chopped onion
    1/2 cup dry vermouth, white wine, or water
    2   cans (7 ounces each) tuna fish packed in water, drained
    3   eggs
  1 1/2 cups buttermilk
    1/4 cup minced fresh parsley
    1/2 teaspoon dried basil
    1/4 teaspoon salt
    3/4 cup grated Parmesan cheese
    1   large tomato, peeled, cut in 6 slices

Cook mushrooms and onion in vermouth in small saucepan over medium heat, covered, 5 minutes. Uncover and cook until vermouth evaporates. Coat 6 individual 1/2-cup ramekins with vegetable cooking spray. Layer tuna and mushroom mixture in 6 individual ramekins, dividing evenly. Beat eggs with buttermilk, parsley, basil, salt, and 1/2 cup cheese in medium bowl; pour over tuna, dividing evenly. Top each ramekin with tomato slice and sprinkle with remaining ¼ cup cheese. Bake in 325° oven 20 to 25 minutes, until set.

BOUILLABAISSE

- 3 cups tomato juice
- 1 cup clam juice
- ½ cup red or white wine
- ¼ cup fresh lemon juice
- 1 small onion, diced
- ½ cup diced celery
- 1 green pepper, diced
- 1 clove garlic, crushed
- 3 tablespoons chopped fresh parsley
- 1 tablespoon oregano

    Shrimp, scallops, chunks of fish, and/or other shellfish as desired, such as clams, or ½ pound filleted fish per person

Combine all ingredients in large pot except seafood and simmer, covered, 30 minutes. Add the seafood. Cook until clams open, fish flakes, and shellfish open.

SEAFOOD ON A SKEWER

Fish

    1-inch chunks fish fillet
    Scallops
    Shrimp

Vegetable/Fruit

    Green pepper chunks
    Small onions or ¼ small onion
    Cherry tomatoes or ¼ tomato
    Mushrooms
    Pineapple chunks
    Mandarin orange sections

Select any of above or substitute preferred fish, fruit, or vegetable. Thread on skewers in alternating combinations. Marinate for 2 hours in combination of:

½   cup fresh lemon juice or ½ cup fresh lime juice, or combination
¼   cup soy or teriyaki sauce
1   clove garlic, mashed, or 1 teaspoon garlic powder
1   tablespoon minced pared fresh gingerroot or 1 teaspoon ground ginger
2   teaspoons honey or equivalent sweetener, plain or brown sugar variety.
1   cup unsweetened pineapple juice (optional)

Broil, bake, or barbecue, basting with marinade.

TUNA PIZZA ON A BAGEL
MAKES 1 SERVING.

½   bagel, dug out
2   ounces tuna fish packed in water, drained
1   tablespoon diced green pepper
1   tablespoon diced onion
1   teaspoon snipped fresh chives
1   teaspoon Lite Way Mayonnaise (page 178)
1   slice tomato
1   slice part-skim mozzarella

Fill bagel with tuna which has been mixed with pepper, onion, chives, mayonnaise. Cover with tomato and mozzarella cheese. Bake in oven or toaster oven until brown and heated through.

TUNA IN PITA
MAKES 1 SERVING.

2   ounces tuna fish packed in water, drained
    Lite Way Mayonnaise (page 178)
1   tablespoon diced onion
⅛   cup alfalfa or bean sprouts
    diced tomato
    Shredded Lettuce
    Small pita bread
1   tablespoon imitation bacon bits

Mix tuna with mayonnaise, onion, sprouts, tomato, and shredded lettuce. Fill small pita bread. Sprinkle with bacon bits.

SOLE ASPARAGUS

MAKES 1 SERVING.

> 5 ounces fillet of sole
> 1/2 cup white wine
> 1 cup cooked or canned white asparagus, drained
> 1/2 medium tomato, chopped
> 1/4 cup evaporated skim-milk
> 1 tablespoon diced pimento
> 1/4 teaspoon onion flakes
>   Salt and pepper to taste

Place fish in a small, nonstick baking dish with 1/2 cup white wine. Bake in 400° oven for 15 to 20 minutes, or until fish flakes easily with fork. In blender container, add half of the asparagus, the tomato, milk, pimento, onion flakes, salt and pepper; process until smooth. Pour into small saucepan. Add wine from fish to saucepan and heat slowly. Do not boil. Remove fish to serving dish. Pour heated sauce over and arrange the remaining asparagus (heated) on top.

GRILLED SHRIMP WITH TARRAGON

MAKES 4 SERVINGS.

> 1 tablespoon fresh lemon juice
> 1 tablespoon soy sauce
> 1 tablespoon dry sherry
> 2 tablespoons vegetable oil
> 1 teaspoon prepared mustard
> 1 teaspoon dried tarragon
> 1 teaspoon chopped fresh parsley
> 1/8 teaspoon pepper
> 1 1/4 pounds of medium shrimp, shelled, deveined, with tails intact

Combine all ingredients except shrimp in bowl and mix. Add shrimp and marinate, covered, overnight. To cook, broil or grill shrimp about 2 minutes on each side. Spoon the marinade over each serving.

POOR BOY LOBSTER
MAKES 4 SERVINGS.

2½ quarts water
3 tablespoons Italian Seasoning (page 24)
1¼ pounds halibut, flounder, or sole, skinned and boned
Lettuce leaves
Lemon wedges
Lime wedges
Lite Way Cocktail Sauce (page 62)

Bring water to boil in large pot. Add seasoning. Cut fish into 4 rectangular pieces. Add to boiling water and simmer for 15-20 minutes. Break into chunks. Serve on lettuce leaves, garnished with lemon and lime wedges, and cocktail sauce.

TARRAGON-BAKED HALIBUT STEAKS
MAKES 2 SERVINGS.

2 halibut steaks (about 5 ounces each)
2 tablespoons fresh lime juice
1 teaspoon tarragon leaves

Brush halibut steaks with lime juice; sprinkle with tarragon leaves. Bake in 400° oven for 10 minutes or until fish flakes easily with a fork.

FISH FILLETS AND CRABMEAT
MAKES 6 SERVINGS.

1 can (7 ounces) crabmeat, drained, boned, flaked
½ cup minced celery
½ teaspoon onion powder
¼ teaspoon salt
Pinch pepper
Pinch dried tarragon
6 small fillets of sole or flounder
¼ cup dry white wine
1½ tablespoons fresh lemon juice
Paprika

Combine crabmeat, celery, onion powder, salt, pepper, and tarragon in bowl. Spread out fish fillets; place a portion of filling, dividing evenly, at one end of each fillet. Roll up fillet and fasten with toothpicks. Place in shallow baking dish; pour wine and lemon juice over fillets. Bake in 325° oven for 20 minutes, basting occasionally. Sprinkle with paprika and serve.

SKEWERED SCALLOPS
MAKES 6 SERVINGS.

- 3/4 cup dry sherry or sake
- 3 tablespoons soy sauce
- 1/2 tablespoon grated pared fresh gingerroot
- 24 sea scallops, rinsed, patted dry with paper towels
- 1 clove garlic, mashed or minced
- 16 dried Chinese black mushrooms

Combine sherry, garlic, soy sauce, and ginger in medium bowl. Add scallops, toss to combine and let stand 2 hours; turn scallops several times while they marinate. Soak mushrooms in warm water to cover for 30 minutes until softened. Remove tough stems and cut softened mushrooms in quarters. Thread scallops and mushrooms on skewers, using 4 scallops and 4 mushrooms for each serving. Broil or grill over low coals until tender, about 5 to 8 minutes. Brush with marinade during cooking and turn skewers several times.

SPICY SOLE
MAKES 4 SERVINGS.

- 2 tablespoons bottled steak sauce
- 1 tablespoon catsup
- 1 tablespoon vinegar (tarragon, cider, or wine)
- 1/4 teaspoon curry powder
- 1 1/4 pounds fillets of sole

Combine all the ingredients except the sole in a small bowl; spread half of mixture on fish and place on heatproof pan coated with vegetable spray. Broil fish about 4 inches from heat for 5 minutes. Turn and spread remaining sauce on fish, and broil 5 minutes longer, until fish flakes easily with fork.

FLOUNDER AU GRATIN
MAKES 4 SERVINGS.

      2   tablespoons grated Parmesan cheese
      1   cup skim milk
      1   teaspoon salt
    1/4   teaspoon pepper
    1/4   teaspoon paprika
      1   pound flounder fillets

Melt cheese with milk in small saucepan. Remove from heat; stir in seasonings. Arrange fillets in baking dish. Spoon sauce evenly over fillets and sprinkle with dash of Parmesan cheese. Bake in 400° oven for 20 minutes, until fish is opaque in center and flakes when tested with a fork.

SHRIMP PARMESAN
MAKES 4 SERVINGS.

    1 1/4   pounds fresh medium shrimp, shelled, deveined
        1   large onion, thinly sliced
      1/2   teaspoon minced garlic
            Pepper to taste
        4   tablespoons grated Parmesan cheese

Coat nonstick skillet with vegetable cooking spray. Cook shrimp and onion in skillet over medium heat stirring constantly until shrimp are pink, about 5 minutes. Sprinkle with garlic, pepper, and Parmesan cheese.

BARBECUED FISH
MAKES 4 SERVINGS.

      1/4   cup water
      1/4   cup catsup
        1   teaspoon Worcestershire sauce
        1   teaspoon fresh lemon juice
        1   onion, sliced
        1   teaspoon dry mustard
      1/2   teaspoon salt
      1/8   teaspoon pepper
    1 1/4   pounds red snapper, bass, or cod fillets or halibut steaks

Combine all the ingredients except fish in a small saucepan and simmer for 5 minutes. Brush fish with sauce. Broil or barbecue fish until it flakes with a fork, basting often with barbecue sauce.

SWORDFISH TERIYAKI
MAKES 6 SERVINGS.

1¼	pounds swordfish steaks
2	tablespoons fresh lemon juice
1	tablespoon soy sauce
½	teaspoon dry mustard
½	teaspoon ground ginger
⅛	teaspoon garlic powder

Place fish steaks in shallow heatproof pan. Combine lemon juice, soy sauce, mustard, ginger, and garlic powder in small bowl. Pour over fish and marinate at room temperature for 1 hour, turning once. Remove fish steaks from marinade and broil 3 inches from heat for 5 minutes. Turn, brush with sauce, and broil 5 to 10 minutes more until fish flakes with a fork.

CRABMEAT IMPERIAL
MAKES 2 SERVINGS

1	head cauliflower
	Salt
1	package (10 ounces) frozen brussel sprouts, or fresh if available
¾	cup skim milk
2	tablespoons grated Sapsago cheese
6	ounces frozen crabmeat, thawed, drained
	Pepper and paprika to taste

Break cauliflower into flowerets and cook in boiling salted water until crisp-tender. Cook sprouts as package directs or, if fresh, in boiling water. Mix milk and cheese in saucepan over low heat, stirring until cheese has melted. Add crabmeat and seasonings. Arrange drained vegetables on platter. Pour crabmeat cream sauce over all and garnish with additional paprika.

❦

FILLET OF SOLE PARMESAN
MAKES 4 SERVINGS

> 1¼ pounds fillet of sole
> ½ teaspoon oregano
> Garlic powder and pepper
> 1 can (8 ounce) tomato sauce
> ½ cup shredded part-skim mozzarella cheese
> 2 tablespoons grated Parmesan cheese

Season fish with oregano, garlic powder, and pepper and place in baking dish coated with vegetable cooking spray. Spread tomato sauce over fish. Sprinkle with cheeses. Bake in 425° oven for 15 minutes.

BUTTERFLY SHRIMP SCAMPI
MAKES 4 SERVINGS.

> 1¼ pounds fresh shrimp, shelled, deveined, but with tails intact
> Artificial butter flavor
> 4 teaspoons fresh grated onion
> Garlic powder
> Finely minced fresh parsley
> Snipped fresh chives
> Paprika
> Juice of 2 lemons

Split each shrimp lengthwise with sharp knife down to tail but leave tail intact. Lay shrimp in shallow heatproof pan in rows, head to tail. Dot each shrimp with butter flavor. Sprinkle grated onion over shrimp. Sprinkle generously with garlic powder, parsley, chives, paprika, and lemon juice. Let shrimp marinate for about 1 hour. Then put pan under broiler for 15 minutes or until tail begins to char and shrimp are done. Serve with juices poured over them.

SCALLOPS TANDOORI STYLE
MAKES 4 SERVINGS.

> ¾ cup plain lowfat yogurt
> 3 tablespoons fresh lime or lemon juice

1   clove garlic, minced
1   teaspoon salt
1/2   teaspoon ground ginger
1/4   teaspoon turmeric
1/4   teaspoon curry powder
1 1/4   pounds large sea scallops
1   teaspoon unsaturated oil
    Paprika

Combine all ingredients except oil and paprika in medium bowl. Mix well to coat scallops evenly. Cover and refrigerate at least 2 hours. Turn scallops occasionally. Thread scallops on skewers and brush lightly with oil. Sprinkle with paprika. Broil or barbecue about 4-inches from heat, turning frequently, for about 8 to 10 minutes.

ROLLED BROCCOLI AND FISH
SERVES 4.

1 1/4   pounds fillets of sole
2   packages (10 ounces each) frozen broccoli spears, cooked, drained (asparagus may be substituted)
1   teaspoon garlic powder
1   teaspoon Lemon Pepper Seasoning (page 24)
1/4   cup dry white wine
1/4   cup sliced green onion
1   tablespoon fresh lemon juice
1   bay leaf
2   tablespoons grated Parmesan cheese
1/2   teaspoon paprika (optional)

Divide fish and broccoli into 4 portions. Sprinkle fillets with 1/4 teaspoon garlic powder and 1/4 teaspoon Lemon Pepper Seasoning. For each portion, wrap fish fillets around broccoli spears. Place rolls in large skillet. Sprinkle with remaining garlic powder and Lemon-Pepper. Combine wine, onion, lemon juice, and bay leaf in small saucepan. Heat to boiling. Pour over fish rolls. Cover and cook slowly for 12 to 15 minutes or until fish flakes with fork. Remove from pan to serving platter. Sprinkle with Parmesan cheese and paprika.

Meat

LONDON BROIL ORIENTALE
MAKES 6 SERVINGS.

- 1¼ pounds flank steak
- 10 tablespoons water
- ½ cup soy sauce
- 2 tablespoons sherry
- ½ teaspoon Tabasco
- 3 cloves garlic, minced
- 1 piece (1 inch) fresh pared gingerroot, grated
- ½ cup minced fresh parsley sprigs (to garnish)

Place steak in a large polyethylene bag. Mix remaining ingredients except parsley in medium bowl; pour over steak in bag and tie securely. Place in a pan and refrigerate several hours or overnight, turning bag occasionally to saturate meat with marinade. Remove broiler pan from oven and turn broiler to high heat. Heat for 15 minutes prior to broiling steak. Remove steak from bag, reserving liquid. Place steak on cold broiler pan on rack and broil about 3-inches from heat for 3 minutes on each side, basting once during broiling with reserved marinade. Heat remaining marinade in small saucepan and pour over meat on heated platter. Garnish with parsley.

STIR FRY BEEF
SERVES 4.

- 1¼ pounds lean round or flank steak, cut into ¼ x 2-inch rounds
- 4 cups sliced fresh mushrooms (about ½ pound)
- 4 cups chopped Chinese cabbage (about 1 head)
- 1 cup sliced bamboo shoots
- 1 cup ½-inch strips celery

¹/₂ cup sliced onion
1   can (4 ounces) water chestnuts, drained, sliced
¹/₂ cup chicken broth or stock
¹/₂ cup sliced green pepper
3   tablespoons soy sauce
3   cups chopped trimmed raw spinach

Heat large nonstick skillet or wok over medium heat and spray with vegetable cooking spray when hot. Add meat and stir fry for about 2 minutes. Push meat to one side. Repeat this procedure with next six ingredients. Add chicken broth. Add green pepper and soy sauce. Stir once and cook for 30 seconds. Combine all ingredients and sprinkle spinach on top. Cover and simmer for 2 minutes.

BEEF AND BROCCOLI STIR FRY
4 SERVINGS.

¹/₃ cup water
2   tablespoons soy sauce
2   tablespoons dry sherry
2   teaspoons grated pared fresh ginger root or 1 teaspoon
      ground ginger
1¹/₂ teaspoons cornstarch
¹/₂ teaspoon minced garlic
¹/₄ teaspoon red pepper flakes
1¹/₄ pounds lean, boneless beef, cut into ¹/₄ x 2-inch strips
1   tablespoon unsaturated oil
4   cups broccoli flowerets

Mix water, soy sauce, sherry, ginger, cornstarch, garlic, and pepper flakes in medium bowl. Add beef; cover and refrigerate for 30 minutes. Put beef mixture in colander over bowl to drain. In wok or large skillet, heat oil over high heat; add beef and stir fry 2 to 3 minutes, until meat has lost pink color. Add broccoli and stir fry 2 to 3 minutes. Add reserved soy sauce marinade and cook 40 to 50 seconds longer, until thickened.

MEAT LOAVES
MAKES 4 SERVINGS.

¹/₂ cup chopped dill pickles
¹/₄ cup Spicy Sauce (recipe follows)
1 tablespoon minced onion
1 tablespoon prepared mustard
1¹/₄ pounds ground lean beef or turkey

Combine pickles, Spicy Sauce, onion flakes, and prepared mustard in small bowl. Divide beef into four equal portions. Flatten each into 4 x 4 inch square. Spoon 2 tablespoons of pickle mixture onto each square. Fold beef over pickles, shaping into oval patties. Cook over hot coals or broil on rack about 4 inches from heat for 8 minutes or until cooked throughout. Turn once during cooking. Serve with remaining pickle mixture and additional Spicy Sauce.

SPICY SAUCE
MAKES 1 CUP.

2 cups tomato juice
2 teaspoons parsley flakes
1 teaspoon barbecue spice
¹/₂ teaspoon dry mustard
¹/₄ teaspoon garlic powder

Combine all ingredients in saucepan. Simmer over moderate heat until mixture is reduced by half. Cool.

HAMBURGER OR VEAL PATTIES
MAKES 1 SERVING.

5 ounces chopped lean beef or veal
2 tablespoons minced onion in 2 tablespoons water or
      bouillon
1 teaspoon minced garlic
1 tablespoon minced celery
¹/₂ teaspoon dried herbs: rosemary, thyme, basil, sage, or dill,
      or 1 teaspoon chopped fresh herbs
   Salt and pepper to taste

Combine meat with herbs in bowl and mix well. Shape into 1 large or 2 small, flat, compact patty (ies). Broil 4 inches from heat, about 5 to 8 minutes on each side. Or, bake on preheated rack in baking dish in 375° oven for about 20 minutes. Rack will allow fat to drip off. Or brown in preheated nonstick skillet until done to taste, turning once.

VEAL SHISH KEBAB
SERVES 4-6.

Marinade:

- ¹/₃ cup soy sauce
- ¹/₃ cup fresh lemon juice
- 1 clove garlic, mashed
- 1 teaspoon mashed pared fresh gingerroot

- 2 pounds boneless leg of veal cut into 1 inch cubes
- 1 pound fresh mushrooms
- 1 green or red pepper, cubed
- 2 onions, peeled, cubed

Combine marinade ingredients in medium bowl. Add meat and vegetables and marinate covered 4 hours or overnight. Thread meat and vegetables alternately on skewers. Broil until brown, 10 to 15 minutes, turning and basting with marinade.

VEAL with MUSHROOMS
SERVES 3-4.

- ¹/₂ teaspoon ground nutmeg
- 1¹/₂ pound boneless veal rump roast tied into compact shape
- 1 cup Lite Way chicken stock (page 26) or bouillon
- ¹/₂ cup dry sherry wine
- 1 cup quartered mushrooms
- 4 teaspoons minced onion
- 2 tablespoons finely chopped fresh parsley

Season meat with nutmeg. Brown meat in large skillet coated with vegetable cooking spray over medium-high heat. Add stock, sherry, mushrooms, and onion. Cover and simmer until meat is tender, about 1 hour. Sprinkle with parsley.

VEAL STROGANOFF
MAKES 3 SERVINGS.

> 1 large onion, diced
> 1 clove garlic, diced
> 1/4 cup chicken stock, bouillon, or Lite Way Stock (page 26)
> 1 1/2 pounds veal cutlets cut into strips
> 1/2 pound fresh mushrooms (4 cups sliced)
> 2/3 cup buttermilk
> 1/4 cup Sauterne
> Salt and pepper to taste

Cook onions and garlic in bouillon in large skillet 3 to 5 minutes. Add veal and mushrooms. Simmer slowly until veal is cooked. Add Sauterne. Simmer 10 minutes. Add buttermilk and salt and pepper. Heat slowly 3 to 5 minutes.

LEMON-BRAISED VEAL STEAK
MAKES 4 SERVINGS.

> 3/4 cup broth or Lite Way Stock (page 26)
> 4 boneless veal steaks from loin or saddle, pounded until 3/4 inch thick
> 1 clove garlic, pressed
> 2 tablespoons fresh lemon juice
> 1/2 teaspoon grated lemon zest
> 1/4 to 1/2 teaspoon salt
> 1/4 teaspoon dried basil leaves
> 1/8 teaspoon pepper
> 1 cup beef stock
> 3/4 cup water

Heat broth in large skillet over moderate high heat; add veal and brown on both sides (4 minutes). Add remaining ingredients and simmer, uncovered, over low heat for 10 minutes, or until veal is fork tender.

VEAL WITH JERUSALEM ARTICHOKES AND TOMATOES
MAKES 4 SERVINGS.

    1   pound stewing veal, trimmed of fat
   3/4 cup stock
    1   onion, chopped fine
    2   cloves garlic, minced
    1   teaspoon rosemary
    2   cups drained canned tomatoes
    1   pound Jerusalem artichokes
        Coarse salt and pepper to taste
    1   tablespoon chopped fresh parsley

Cook pieces of veal in stock in large skillet; add onion, garlic, rosemary, tomatoes. Cover and simmer for 45 minutes. Peel and trim Jerusalem artichokes and cut into 1/2-inch-thick slices. Add to veal, season with salt and pepper, and cover and cook another 20 minutes or until artichokes are done. Garnish with parsley and serve.

VEAL SCALLOPINI
MAKES 1 SERVING.

    4   to 5 large mushrooms, sliced
    4   ounces veal, cut into strips, pounded thin
        Juice of 1/2 lemon
    1   teaspoon garlic powder
        Dash pepper
   1/2 cup beef stock
    2   tablespoons dry vermouth
    2   teaspoons chopped fresh parsley

Sauté mushrooms in skillet coated with vegetable cooking spray for 15 minutes over medium heat. Remove from pan. Sprinkle veal with a few drops of lemon juice, garlic powder, and pepper. Sauté veal quickly over medium-high heat about 2 to 3 minutes on each side, until lightly browned. Remove to warm serving platter. Return mushrooms to pan. Add beef stock, remaining lemon juice, and vermouth. Reduce over high heat, scraping up brown drippings from bottom of pan. Sprinkle with chopped parsley. Pour over veal and serve.

VEAL-STUFFED CABBAGE

MAKES 4 SERVINGS.

1 large head cabbage, cored, separated into leaves
1 onion, sliced
1½ pounds extra-lean ground veal
1 tablespoon rice
1¼ cups water
½ teaspoon minced garlic
¼ teaspoon seasoned salt
¼ teaspoon pepper
1 can (8 ounces) tomato sauce
¼ cup seedless raisins
   Artificial sweetener to taste
2 tablespoons fresh lemon juice

Steam or cook cabbage in small amount of water until crisp-tender. In nonstick skillet coated with vegetable cooking spray, sauté half the onions until lightly browned. Add veal, rice, ¼ cup water, garlic, seasoned salt, and pepper. Cook until veal is browned and crumbly. Place some meat mixture on each cabbage leaf. Roll into cylinders, tucking in ends; secure with toothpicks. Combine tomato sauce, 1 cup water, and remaining onion in small bowl. Arrange cabbage rolls in 2½ qt. baking dish and pour sauce over rolls. Cover and bake in 350° oven for 1 hour. Add raisins, sweetener, and lemon juice. Cook, uncovered, 30 minutes longer.

VEAL AL LIMONE

MAKES 4 SERVINGS.

1¼ pounds veal scallops, pounded thin (¼ inch)
1 teaspoon salt
½ teaspoon pepper
¾ cup beef bouillon or stock
1 tablespoon fresh lemon juice
¼ cup chopped fresh parsley
½ lemon, thinly sliced

Season veal with salt and pepper. Brown veal in nonstick pan coated with vegetable cooking spray for approximately 10 minutes turning frequently so meat is evenly browned. Transfer veal to baking dish. Combine bouillon, lemon juice and parsley in small bowl; slowly pour down side of dish. Place lemon slices over veal. Cover. Bake in 325° oven for 20 minutes.

CHILI WITH VEAL
SERVES 4.

1¼ pounds extra lean ground veal
1 large onion, chopped
1½ teaspoons chili powder
½ teaspoon salt
½ teaspoon garlic powder
½ teaspoon dried oregano
¼ teaspoon pepper
¼ teaspoon cumin
1 can (7½ ounces) tomatoes
⅔ cup canned tomato purée

Brown veal in nonstick skillet coated with vegetable cooking spray. Drain off all fat. Add onion and cook. Add chili, salt, garlic powder, oregano, pepper, cumin, tomatoes, and purée. Heat to boiling, stirring well. Reduce heat; cover and simmer for 45 to 60 minutes.

VEAL ROAST
MAKES 6 SERVINGS.

2 to 2½ pounds boned, rolled veal roast
1 teaspoon salt
1 teaspoon oregano
3 cloves of garlic, slivered
2 tablespoons chopped fresh parsley
1 small onion, slivered

Place roast on bed of oregano and onion. Mix garlic, parsley, and salt in small bowl. Poke holes in roast and fill with garlic mixture. Roast in 300° oven 25 minutes per pound.

SLOPPY JOE
MAKES 4 SERVINGS.

1¼ pounds ground hamburger meat
1   onion, chopped
1   teaspoon salt
¼   teaspoon pepper
1   6 ounce can tomato paste
1   8 ounce can tomato sauce
2   cups tomato juice
    Artificial sweetener to taste
½   teaspoon prepared mustard
¼   teaspoon Worcestershire sauce

Mix meat, onion, salt, and pepper together in bowl. Brown in frying pan about 12-15 minutes over medium high heat, stirring meat constantly. Drain off all fat. Then add remaining ingredients. Simmer over low heat for 20 minutes until heated through and liquid reduces so mixture thickens.

CHOPPED CHICKEN LIVERS
MAKES 4 SERVINGS AS APPETIZER.

½   cup plus 2 to 3 tablespoons chicken stock
2   small onions, sliced
½   pound chicken livers
2   hard-cooked eggs, chopped
½   teaspoon salt
    Pepper to taste

Heat ½ cup stock in skillet; add onion and cook until tender, about 10 minutes. Broil chicken livers until brown. Chop livers finely. Mix onions, livers, egg, salt and pepper to taste. Add 2 tablespoons stock to moisten mixture.

VEAL AND PEPPERS
MAKES 4 SERVINGS.

1   pound veal scallopini (8 slices)
1   large onion, chopped
1   green pepper, chopped
    Paprika

    1   tablespoon grated garlic
   3/4 cup beef bouillon or beef/veal Lite Way Stock (page 26)
    1   tomato, chopped

Place veal slices on flat surface and pound with bottom of clean heavy skillet. Brown veal in skillet coated with vegetable cooking spray; remove and set aside. Simmer onions and peppers with paprika and garlic in bouillon in same pan. Add tomato. Cook for 1 to 2 minutes. Return veal to pan and heat through 1 minute.

VEAL CHOPS L'ORANGE
MAKES 2 SERVINGS.

    2   veal loin chops
    1   teaspoon salt
   1/2 teaspoon paprika
   1/2 cup beef bouillon or Lite Way Beef/Veal Stock (page 26)
    1   tablespoon snipped fresh chives
    1   orange, peeled, diced

Sprinkle veal chops with salt and paprika. Cut one horizontal slit in each chop, forming a pocket. Brown them on both sides in nonstick pan. Transfer to baking dish. Pour bouillon over chops. Combine chives and orange in small bowl. Spoon half the mixture evenly into slit in each chop; place any leftover mixture on top of chops. Bake in 325° oven for 20 minutes, until tender.

VEAL PARMESAN #1
MAKES 1 SERVING.

    4   ounces veal scallopini, cut into 1/4-inch-thick slices, 3 x 3
          inches wide
    1   tablespoon grated Parmesan cheese
   1/4 cup skim milk
    1   slice part-skim mozzarella or Muenster cheese
    1   cup Marinara Sauce (page 126)

Place veal slices between wax paper on flat surface and pound thin with heavy skillet. Dip veal in milk. Coat with Parmesan cheese. Place in baking dish and bake uncovered in 350° oven for 20 minutes. Top with mozzarella cheese. Pour Marinara Sauce over veal and cheese. Bake 10 minutes longer, or until cheese melts.

VEAL PARMESAN #2
MAKES 1 SERVING.

1   can (8 ounces) tomato sauce
2   teaspoons garlic powder
1   teaspoon marjoram
1   teaspoon oregano
1   teaspoon grated Parmesan cheese
1   garlic clove, crushed
4   ounces veal scallopini, sliced and pounded per Veal
      Parmesan #1
2   slices part-skim mozzarella cheese (each slice 1 ounce)

Combine tomato sauce, garlic powder, marjoram, and oregano in small saucepan and simmer 10 minutes. Brown garlic 2-3 minutes in nonstick skillet coated with vegetable cooking spray. Add veal, brown over high heat 30 seconds on each side. Transfer to baking dish. Cover cutlet with sauce. Place mozzarella on cutlet. Sprinkle Parmesan cheese over top. Bake in 325° oven until cheese melts, 3-5 minutes.

Sauces

Butter, cream, margarine, meat drippings, and oils in gravies and sauces—the fat calories—are the enemies of the Lite Way. Nor does one need extra flour and cornstarch or canned cream soup (250 + calories) as thickeners.

When ½ cup cream or other rich thickener is called for in sauces or casseroles, try ¼ cup evaporated skimmed milk, ½ cup buttermilk, or nonfat dry milk which adds only 40 to 60 calories. One-half cup of sour cream, half-and-half, or light cream adds 160 to 240 calories.

LITE WAY TIPS

1. Remove fat from meat drippings by mixing with ice cubes! Fat will cling to cubes. Remove cubes.
2. Simmer stock to "reduce" amount and thicken. Vegetable purées can also be used to thicken when appropriate.
3. For cream sauces, use canned evaporated skim milk, buttermilk, or yogurt instead of cream or sour cream.
4. Use butter flavoring instead of butter.
5. Use wine and herbs for flavor; 85% of the calories in wine will cook off.

MARINARA SAUCE
MAKES 6 CUPS.

1	can (46 ounce) tomato juice
1	cup Lite Way "sautéed" onion, chopped
2	green peppers, chopped
1	red pepper, chopped
2	basil leaves, minced
1	clove garlic, minced
½	pound mushrooms, sliced
½	teaspoon oregano
1	cup bouillon or Lite Way stock (optional)

Combine all the ingredients except the mushrooms and oregano in medium saucepan. Cook, uncovered, for about 45 minutes. During last 10 minutes, add mushrooms and oregano, and a little bouillon, if desired. Will keep in refrigerator for 2 weeks if stored in tight glass container. Excellent with veal, chicken, fish, and eggs.

BARBEQUE SAUCE
MAKES ¾ CUP.

¼	cup vinegar
¼	cup water
¼	cup tomato catsup
1	tablespoon chopped onion
1	teaspoon Worcestershire sauce
1	teaspoon fresh lemon juice
½	teaspoon dry mustard

Combine all ingredients in small saucepan. Simmer 1 hour to blend seasonings. Store in refrigerator. Brush on steaks, burgers, chops, or roasts during grilling.

CHILI SAUCE

MAKES 3 CUPS.

2 pounds tomatoes, peeled, chopped
6 stalks celery, chopped
1 cup chopped onion
1 red pepper, chopped
1 green pepper, chopped
1 teaspoon mustard seed
1 teaspoon celery seed
1 stick cinnamon
3 whole cloves
2 cups cider vinegar
2 teaspoons salt
2 tablespoons or less artificial liquid sweetener

Combine chopped tomatoes, celery, onion, green and red peppers in large heavy saucepan. Cover and simmer for 1 hour. Tie mustard seed, celery seed, cinnamon stick, and cloves in cheesecloth to make spice bag. Simmer 2 more hours with spice bag, vinegar, and salt added. Remove spice bag. Stir in sweetener. Cool, then pour in sterilized jars and cover. Keep refrigerated. Serve with cold meat.

DESSERTS

There are times when you want something rich—for company, or for a treat. Lite Way dessert recipes—even some for chocolate desserts—fill that need and keep the calories low at the same time.

The surest way to eat Lite Way is to eliminate cakes and pies from your dessert menus. Instead, eat fruits, melons and berries. They are so sweet you don't even have to add sweeteners.

Everyone knows that yogurt is a low-calorie food, but don't let it fool you when it goes into partnership. Before you reach for fruited yogurt on the supermarket shelf, check the label: calories may range from 150 to 270 according to brand.

Also, before you order a big dish of frozen yogurt with "natural" toppings, take a look at how naturally high in calories they are:

Topping	Calories
½ cup coconut chips	165
¾ cup banana chips	300
¼ cup wheat germ	110
¼ cup slivered almonds	360
½ cup of granola	275
1 cup sunflower seeds	205
15 walnut halves	195

GENERAL SUGGESTIONS FOR LITE WAY DESSERTS

1. Are you the average American who uses over 120 pounds of sugar a year (often hidden) . . . that is 180,000 unnecessary calories a year.
2. Use beaten egg whites combined with fruit to make luscious whips.
3. Use plain gelatin instead of Jello in dessert recipes, adding fruit for sweetness and flavor.

4. Make cheesecake with cottage cheese instead of cream cheese.

5. Season baked apples or pears with cinnamon and fresh lemon juice instead of sugar.

6. Use a spoonful of vanilla yogurt instead of whipped cream as a topping.

7. Add exotic fruits such as kiwi and papaya to fruit compote.

8. Splurge with a few raspberries to sparkle a fruit cup.

9. Serve whips or compotes in a scooped out orange or pineapple shell.

10. Sugar by any other name—dextrose, sucrose, corn syrup, honey, molasses—still adds up to 16 calories per teaspoon.

11. Use fresh fruit whenever you can. This is the reason:

Pineapple	*Calories*
1½ cups fresh pineapple	80
1½ cups pineapple in natural juice	140
1½ cups pineapple in heavy syrup.	190
1½ cups *lite* pineapple.	120

Fruit Desserts

COFFEE BAKED APPLES
MAKES 5 SERVINGS.

5	baking apples, cored
1	cup orange juice
1	tablespoon instant coffee granules
1½	teaspoons brown sweetener
¼	teaspoon ground cinnamon

Peel top half of each stemmed and cored apple. Place in 8-inch square pan; set aside. In small bowl, mix orange juice, coffee granules, sweetener, and cinnamon. Pour over apples. Bake in preheated 350° oven 50 to 55 minutes, basting occasionally.

BROILED ORANGE HALVES
MAKES 2 SERVINGS.

1	medium orange
¼	teaspoon ground cinnamon
¼	teaspoon ground mace

Cut orange in half crosswise; remove seeds, if any. With small sharp knife cut around each section. Sprinkle each half with cinnamon and mace. Broil 7 minutes or until golden and hot.

FRUIT SORBET

In plastic freezer bags or freezer foil, freeze very ripe, peeled, cut up bananas and pineapples, cut up peaches with peels, plums, and berries. Feed solidly frozen fruit through juicer to make sorbet. Combine whatever fruit desired.

MELON FRUIT CUP
MAKES 1 SERVING.

- ½ melon
- 4 strawberries
- ¼ cup blueberries
- ½ cup fresh grapefruit sections
- ½ plum, cut up
  Cinnamon or freshly grated nutmeg

Cut melon meat into bite-size pieces, reserving shell, and combine with remaining fruits. Sprinkle with cinnamon or nutmeg and spoon mixture into melon shell.

FRUIT YOGURT MELANGE
MAKES 2 SERVINGS.

- 1 cup plain lowfat yogurt
- ½ banana, sliced
- 1 teaspoon raisins or ½ cup cherries, pitted
  Artificial sweetener

Mix all the ingredients in medium bowl.

ORANGE-APPLE SMOOTHIE
MAKES 4 SERVINGS.

- 8 ounces orange juice
- 2 medium apples, peeled, cored, diced

Combine orange juice and apple in blender container; run at medium speed for 2 minutes or until mixture is smooth. Pour into freezer tray; freeze until firm. To serve, let mixture soften at room temperature for 30 minutes. Stir well until mixture is consistency of sherbet. Serve in bowl.

GOURMET FRUIT

>Chunks of fresh pineapple or fresh strawberries or other
>   fruit
>Plain or vanilla low-fat yogurt
>Ground cinnamon

Mix any unsweetened fresh or fresh frozen fruit with enough plain yogurt in small bowl to thoroughly coat fruit when tossed. Allow to set and chill. Serve in wine goblet with sprinkle of cinnamon.

COTTAGE PARFAIT

>Lowfat cottage cheese
>Fresh or fresh frozen fruit

Alternate layers of lowfat cottage cheese with fresh or frozen strawberries, blueberries, and raspberries or other fruit in tall parfait glasses.

CINNAMON BAKED APPLES
MAKES 4 SERVINGS.

>4 apples
>2 cups water
>1 teaspoon ground cinnamon
>2 teaspoons vanilla extract
>   Artificial sweetener equal to ⅓ cup sugar
>   Plain lowfat yogurt

Wash and core apples. Remove peeling from top one-third of apple. Arrange apples in baking dish. Combine water, cinnamon, vanilla, and sugar substitute in small saucepan; heat to boiling, and pour over apples. Bake apples in 350° oven for 1 hour or until tender. Serve hot or cold with plain yogurt and sprinkle cinnamon on top of yogurt.

YOGURT AND FRESH FRUIT
MAKES 6 SERVINGS.

1 small ripe banana, mashed
1 orange, peeled, sectioned
1 cup cut up fresh pineapple
1 cup plain lowfat yogurt

Combine fruit with yogurt in medium bowl.

BRANDIED PEACHES
MAKES 4 SERVINGS.

8 canned peach halves with ½ cup unsweetened juice
Brown sugar substitute equal to ¼ cup brown sugar or less
8 to 10 whole cloves
1 cinnamon stick
½ teaspoon brandy extract

Combine all ingredients except extract in saucepan. Cover and simmer 4 to 6 minutes. Remove from heat. Add extract. Serve warm or chilled, after removing cloves.

LUMPY APPLESAUCE
MAKES 6 SERVINGS.

4 apples
½ cup water
1 teaspoon fresh lemon juice
1 teaspoon ground cinnamon
⅛ teaspoon freshly grated nutmeg
Artificial sweetener to taste
1 tablespoon plain or vanilla lowfat yogurt

Peel, core, and cut apples into chunks. Combine with water and spices in saucepan. Heat to boiling. Simmer 5 to 10 minutes checking so that some apples are still firm. If desired, sweeten with a little artificial sweetener. Mix and serve warm or cold with 1 tablespoon plain yogurt and cinnamon or 1 tablespoon vanilla yogurt.

BAKED APPLE IN CHERRY SAUCE
MAKES 1 SERVING.

   1 apple
  1/4 cup cherry diet soda

Core apple. Put apple in baking pan and fill center with soda. Bake in 350° oven for 30 minutes.

ORANGE SHERBET
MAKES 1 SERVING.

  1/3 cup nonfat dry milk
   2 cups orange juice

Mix milk and juice in bowl. Pour into ice cube tray and place in freezer until slightly frozen. Transfer to bowl and beat until smooth and creamy. Return to tray and freeze slightly. Defrost a little to serve.

PINEAPPLE ORANGE FREEZE
MAKES 8 SERVINGS.

     Orange Sherbet (preceding recipe)
  1 medium pineapple
  2 medium bananas
  2 tablespoons brandy or rum extract

Make orange sherbet. Cut pineapple in half lengthwise. Cut out all pulp and dice it. Reserve shell. Peel and slice bananas. Combine pineapple and bananas with extract in bowl; stuff shell with fruit mixture. Serve in fruit dishes. Top each with scoop of sherbet.

FRUITSICLE
MAKES 4 SERVINGS.

  1/2 medium pineapple, peeled, diced.
   1 cup orange juice
  1/8 teaspoon ground cloves
   4 cinnamon sticks

Blend pineapple, orange juice, and cloves in blender at medium speed for 2 minutes or until mixture is smooth. Pour one quarter of mixture into each of 4 paper cups. Chill in freezer for 40 minutes or until mixture is half frozen. Insert cinnamon stick into center of each cup. Freeze until firm. To serve, remove from freezer and tear paper cup away from pop. Use cinnamon stick as holder.

STRAWBERRY FRAPPE POPS
MAKES 6 SERVINGS.

- 1 cup buttermilk
- 1 cup strawberries
- Artificial sweetener to taste

Blend buttermilk and strawberries in blender at medium speed until berries are puréed. Add sweetener. Blend 2 more minutes. Pour into pop molds. Freeze until firm, at least 2 hours. Before serving, dip molds into warm water to loosen pops.

MOCK "CARVEL"
MAKES 1 SERVING.

- ⅓ cup nonfat dry milk
- ⅓ cup cherry diet soda
- 1 envelope artificial sweetener
- 5 fresh or frozen strawberries

Mix milk powder, soda, strawberries and sweetener in bowl until smooth. Place in freezer for ½ hour.

BANANA YOGURT SUNDAE
MAKES 2 SERVINGS.

- ½ small banana, mashed
- ⅔ cup plain lowfat yogurt
- 1 teaspoon lemon extract
- Artificial sweetener to taste

Blend mashed banana with yogurt in small bowl. Stir in extract. Chill.

ALTERNATE FRUIT YOGURTS
EACH MAKES 1 SERVING.

Add to ⅔ cup plain low-fat yogurt:

    ½   cup applesauce, ground cinnamon, freshly grated nutmeg, ground cloves

        OR

    ½   cup strawberries

        OR

    ⅓   cup pitted cherries

        OR

Harlequin Parfait

    ⅔   cup plain lowfat yogurt
    ¼   cup sliced strawberries
    ¼   banana, sliced
    ¼   peach, sliced
    1   teaspoon fresh lemon juice

Alternate yogurt with fruit slices and lemon juice in glass dish.

APPLE CHEWS
MAKES 4 SERVINGS.

    1   cup nonfat dry milk
    3   tablespoons flour
    ¾   teaspoon ground cinnamon
    ¾   teaspoon baking powder
        Artificial sweetener to taste
  1½   medium apples, peeled, cored, and grated
    ¾   teaspoon vanilla extract

Combine dry milk, flour, cinnamon, baking powder and sweetener in small bowl. Add apple and vanilla; stir until blended and moistened. Divide mixture into 4 portions. Drop each one, from a spoon, about 2 inches apart, on nonstick baking sheet coated with vegetable cooking spray. Wet back of spoon by dipping in water. Flatten each portion by pressing with wet spoon to about ¼ inch thickness. Bake in 375° oven about 10 to 12 minutes or until golden. Cool on wire rack.

PUMPKIN APPLE THINS
MAKES 2 SERVINGS.

  1 apple
  ½ cup canned pumpkin
     Artificial sweetener to taste
  ½ teaspoon ground cinnamon
  ¼ teaspoon freshly grated nutmeg
  ⅔ cup nonfat dry milk
  ½ teaspoon almond extract
     Cinnamon topping (recipe follows)

Core and grate apple. Combine with remaining ingredients except Cinnamon Topping in bowl. Drop by teaspoonfuls on nonstick baking sheet coated with vegetable cooking spray. Flatten with back of spoon. Bake in 375° oven for 20 minutes. Remove from oven. Sprinkle with Cinnamon Topping. Serve warm.

CINNAMON TOPPING

     Artificial sweetener to taste
  1 teaspoon ground cinnamon

Combine ingredients in shaker.

APPLE WHIP
MAKES 3 SERVINGS.

  ⅔ cup nonfat dry milk
  ½ cup cold water
     Juice of 1 lemon
  1 cup unsweetened applesauce
  ½ teaspoon vanilla extract
  ⅛ teaspoon ground cinnamon
     Pinch freshly grated nutmeg

Combine dry milk powder with cold water in small bowl and allow to stand, covered, in refrigerator for 1 hour or more. Add lemon juice; beat until consistency of whipped cream. Stir in applesauce, vanilla, cinnamon, and nutmeg. Chill and serve.

LEMON PIE
MAKES 3 SERVINGS.

> 3 medium eggs, separated
>   Artificial sweetener to taste
> 2 tablespoons cold water
>   Juice and grated zest of 1 lemon
>   Dash of salt

Beat egg yolks with pinch of sweetener. Stir in water and lemon juice and zest. Cook in top of double boiler over simmering water until thick. Remove from heat. Add salt and sweetener to taste to egg whites; beat until stiff. Fold into hot egg yolk mixture. Fill 8-inch nonstick pie plate. Bake in 350° oven until top is lightly browned.

MOCHA POPS
MAKES 10 POPS.

> 2   envelopes unflavored gelatin
> 1/2 cup cold black coffee
> 2   cups hot black coffee
> 1   cup nonfat dry milk
>   Artificial sweetener to equal 1/4 cup sugar
> 1   teaspoon vanilla extract
> 1   teaspoon chocolate extract

Sprinkle gelatin over cold coffee in small bowl. Stir to dissolve. Add hot coffee and stir to dissolve. Add 1/3 cup of the dry milk, the sweetener, and extracts; stir. Refrigerate until firm. When firm, process in blender with remaining dry milk until smooth. Freeze in 3 ounce paper cups 10 minutes. Insert wooden sticks. Freeze until firm.

WATERMELON SHERBET
MAKES 4 SERVINGS.

> 4 cups cubed seeded watermelon
> 2 tablespoons fresh lemon juice
>   Artificial sweetener

Purée all ingredients in blender. Pour into ice cube tray with insert and freeze for 1 or 2 hours, until cubes are crystalized. Return cubes to blender and purée again, scraping down sides with spatula if necessary. Divide evenly into sherbet glasses and return to freezer to set.

PEACH MELBA
MAKES 4 SERVINGS.

> 4 medium peaches, blanched, and peeled
> 1 teaspoon vanilla extract
> 1 cup raspberries, or ¾ teaspoon raspberry extract
>   Artificial sweetener to taste
>   Whipped Topping (page 153)

Cut peaches in half and remove pits. Place on individual dishes. Sprinkle vanilla over peaches. In bowl, mash berries with sweetener. (Or mix extract with sweetener.) Spoon over peach halves. Refrigerate while preparing topping. Spoon topping over peaches and chill.

GRAPEFRUIT
MAKES 2 SERVINGS.

> 1 grapefruit
>   Diet cherry soda

Cut grapefruit in half, pour a little diet cherry soda over each half, and place under broiler for a few minutes.

POACHED WHOLE PEARS
MAKES 4 SERVINGS.

> 4 ripe small pears
> 1 cup citrus-flavored diet soda
> 1 piece lemon rind
> 1 small piece cinnamon stick
>   Artificial sweetener to taste

Peel skin from top half of pears. In saucepan, combine fruit with remaining ingredients except sweetener and simmer until soft.

Remove fruit to platter. Quickly cook liquid until reduced by half; stir in sweetener and pour sauce over fruit. Serve hot or chilled.

APPLE FOAM
MAKES 4 SERVINGS.

- 2 cups grated peeled apples
- 3 tablespoons fresh lemon juice
  Artificial sweetener to taste
  Dash of salt
  Dash of freshly grated nutmeg
- 3 egg whites
- 1/4 cup confectioners sugar
- 1/4 teaspoon ground cinnamon

Combine grated apple, lemon juice, sweetener, salt, and nutmeg in bowl. Beat egg whites in another bowl until soft peaks form. Beat in confectioner's sugar until stiff peaks form. Gently fold in apple mixture. Sprinkle with cinnamon and serve immediately.

GRAPEFRUIT WHIP
MAKES 3 SERVINGS.

- 2 tablespoons unflavored gelatin
- 1 1/2 cups unsweetened grapefruit juice
- 2 tablespoons fresh lemon juice
- 1/2 teaspoon ground cinnamon
  Artificial sweetener to taste
- 1 cups coarsely crushed ice

Combine gelatin and 1/2 cup grapefruit juice in small pan. Heat to boiling, stirring to dissolve, and pour into blender. Process at high speed for 30 seconds. Add remaining grapefruit juice, lemon juice, cinnamon, and sweetener. Run at high speed for 30 seconds. Add ice. Run at medium speed for 1 minute or until mixture is smooth. Pour into bowl or serving dishes. Chill until set.

APPLE SNOW

MAKES 1 SERVING.

  1 teaspoon unflavored gelatin
  ¼ cup boiling water
  2 teaspoons fresh lemon juice
  ½ cup unsweetened applesauce; or 1 small peach, mashed; or
        ½ small banana, mashed
     Artificial sweetener to taste
  1 egg white

Sprinkle gelatin over boiling water and stir to dissolve. Add lemon juice. Chill until set. Add fruit and a few drops of liquid sweetener. Beat egg white until stiff. Fold into gelatin-fruit mixture. Chill.

ORANGE SNOW

MAKES 3-4 SERVINGS.

  1 envelope unflavored gelatin
  1 cup orange juice
     Artificial sweetener equal to ¼ cup sugar
  2 tablespoons fresh lemon juice
     Dash of salt
  4 egg whites at room temperature
     Orange sections (optional)
     Fresh mint leaves (optional)

Sprinkle gelatin over orange juice in small pan, to soften; let stand 5 minutes. Heat to boiling. Remove from heat. Add half the sweetener; stir. Pour into bowl. Add lemon juice. Set bowl in large bowl of ice cubes to chill, stirring occasionally, until as thick as unbeaten egg white, about 10 minutes. Add salt to egg whites; beat until foamy. Gradually add rest of sweetener, beating well. Continue beating until soft peaks form. Using same beaters, beat gelatin mixture until foamy. Fold egg whites into gelatin. Turn into 4-cup oiled mold; refrigerate about 2 hours, or until set. To unmold: run a spatula around edge of mold. Invert over serving plate. Place hot, damp dishcloth over mold; shake to release. If desired, garnish with orange sections and fresh mint leaves.

FRESH FRUIT IN PINEAPPLE SHELL
MAKES 8 SERVINGS.

> 1   medium ripe pineapple
> ¼   cup unsweetened grapefruit juice
> 1   cup fresh strawberries
> 1   cup seedless green grapes, halved
>   Fresh mint leaves

Cut a 1½-inch thick slice from top and bottom of pineapple. Set slices aside. With long, narrow knife, remove pineapple from shell in one piece, leaving shell intact. Cut pineapple lengthwise into 12 spears. Remove and discard core from pineapple. Cut pineapple into chunks; place chunks in large bowl. Add grapefruit juice; mix gently. Refrigerate, covered, for 3 hours.

Meanwhile, wash strawberries; drain. Reserve a few berries for garnish. Hull remaining berries, and slice. Refrigerate along with grapes. Just before serving, toss sliced strawberries and grapes with pineapple. Set pineapple shell on reserved bottom slice in shallow dish. Spoon chilled fruit into shell. Garnish with reserved whole berries, fresh mint, and pineapple frond.

ORANGE STRAWBERRY FREEZE
MAKES 2 SERVINGS.

> ½   cup orange juice
> 1   cup frozen strawberries
>   Artificial sweetener to taste

Purée all ingredients in blender until smooth. Pour into freezer tray and freeze until firm.

CHERRY YOGURT POPS
MAKES 4 SERVINGS.

> 1   cup plain lowfat yogurt
> 20   large fresh or frozen pitted cherries
> 1   teaspoon fresh lemon juice
>   Artificial sweetener to taste

Purée all ingredients in blender until smooth. Divide evenly into four plastic freezer containers. Freeze until crystals form. Insert wooden skewer in center of each. Freeze until firm (about 3/4 hour). Remove from containers.

STRAWBERRY PARISIENNE
MAKES 1 SERVING.

- ½ teaspoon vanilla extract
- ½ cup Whipped Topping (page 153)
- ½ cup strawberries, sliced

Stir vanilla into strawberries, in small bowl. Fold strawberries into topping. Serve in sherbet glasses.

PINEAPPLE-STRAWBERRY FRIBBLE
MAKES 4 SERVINGS.

- ¼ cup cold water
- 1 envelope unflavored gelatin
- ½ cup hot unsweetened pineapple juice
- 1 envelope Alba 77 Strawberry flavor
  Artificial sweetener to taste
- 2½ cups crushed ice

Combine water and gelatin in blender. Allow gelatin to soften 2-3 minutes. Blend 30 seconds. Add pineapple juice, Alba 77, and sweetener; blend 30 seconds. Add ice; blend 30 seconds. Spoon into dessert dishes.

COCOPINE
MAKES 2 SERVINGS.

- 1 cup cold evaporated skim milk
- 1 cup cold water
- ½ cup canned crushed pineapple, no sugar added
- ½ teaspoon rum extract
- ½ teaspoon coconut extract
- ¼ teaspoon vanilla extract
  Artificial sweetener to taste
- 4 ice cubes

Combine all ingredients except ice cubes in blender; process until smooth. Add ice cubes, one at a time, until all ice is crushed.

BANANA FLUFF

MAKES 2 SERVINGS.

 1   envelope unflavored gelatin
 1/4 cup cold water
 1/4 cup boiling water
 1   small ripe banana, divided
 2/3 cup nonfat dry milk
 1/2 teaspoon coconut extract
     Artificial sweetener to taste
 6   to 8 ice cubes

Sprinkle gelatin over cold water in blender container. Add boiling water; process to dissolve gelatin. Add three-quarters of the banana, the milk, coconut extract, and sweetener. Process until smooth. Add ice, slowly. Dice remaining banana; fold into blended mixture. Divide into 2 dessert glasses. Serve or chill.

STRAWBERRY FLUFF

MAKES 4 SERVINGS.

 1/2 cup cold water
 1   cup reconstituted nonfat dry milk, hot
 1   envelope Alba 77 Vanilla flavor
 1   envelope unflavored gelatin
     Artificial sweetener to taste
 1 1/2 teaspoons vanilla extract
 2   egg yolks
 1 1/4 cups crushed ice
 1   cup fresh strawberries

In blender, combine water and gelatin. Allow 2-3 minutes for gelatin to soften. Blend 30 seconds. Add hot milk, Alba 77, sweetener, vanilla, and egg yolks. Blend 30 seconds. With motor running, add ice; continue to blend 30 seconds. Pour into 1-quart serving dish. Chill until set. Garnish with strawberries.

CANTALOUPE SUPREME
MAKES 4 SERVINGS.

    1   medium cantaloupe, halved, seeded
    1   cup skim milk
    1   teaspoon vanilla extract
        Artificial sweetener to taste

With melon baller, scoop out each half of cantaloupe, leaving two thin shells; reserve shells. Combine skim milk, extract, and sweetener in small bowl. Pour over melon balls in medium bowl. Refrigerate at least 1 hour. To serve, spoon half of balls and liquid into each reserved shell.

LEMON CREAM
MAKES 1 SERVING.

    1   medium egg, separated
    1   cup lemon-lime diet soda
    2   tablespoons fresh lemon juice
    1   envelope unflavored gelatin
        Artificial sweetener to taste

In small pan, combine egg yolk, soda, lemon juice, and gelatin. Cook over low heat, stirring, until gelatin dissolves and lemon mixture thickens slightly; do not boil. Pour into an individual ½ cup soufflé dish; cool. Beat egg white and sweetener until stiff but not dry. Place mounds of egg white on lemon mixture; spread to edge of dish. With back of spoon, pull up points of meringue. Bake in 425° oven, 3 to 4 minutes or until slightly browned.

STRAWBERRY CHEESE MOUSSE
MAKES 4 SERVINGS.

    1⅓   cups lowfat cottage cheese
     ¾   cup nonfat dry milk
     ¾   cup water
     2   tablespoons fresh lemon juice
     ½   teaspoon vanilla extract
     ½   teaspoon salt
         Artificial sweetener to taste
     2   envelopes unflavored gelatin
     2   cups strawberries, sliced

Purée cheese, milk, ½ cup water, lemon juice, vanilla extract, salt, and sweetener in blender until smooth. Transfer to bowl. Pour rest of water into pan. Sprinkle gelatin over water to soften, about 5 minutes. Place over low heat, stirring until dissolved. Pour into cheese mixture and mix well. Fold in strawberries. Pour into oiled bombe mold and chill until set.

SPANISH CREAM
MAKES 2 SERVINGS.

> 1 teaspoon unflavored gelatin
> 1 cup skim milk
>   Pinch salt
> 1 egg, separated
>   Artificial sweetener to taste
> ½ teaspoon vanilla extract

Sprinkle gelatin over milk in top of double boiler to soften for 5 minutes. Add salt. Stir over boiling water until gelatin is dissolved; remove from heat. Beat egg yolk in small bowl; gradually pour milk over yolk, stirring constantly. Stir in sweetener. Return mixture to top of double boiler and cook, stirring constantly, over hot, not boiling, water until mixture coats back of spoon. Chill in refrigerator until thick and syrupy. Beat egg white until stiff. Add vanilla and fold beaten egg white into egg yolk mixture. Pour into two dessert dishes and chill until set. Serve plain or with fruit.

CUSTARD
MAKES 2 SERVINGS.

> ⅔ cup skim milk
> 1 egg
> ⅛ teaspoon salt
> 2 drops vanilla extract
>   Ground nutmeg
>   Artificial sweetener to taste

Scald milk in small saucepan; cool slightly. Beat egg; add with salt and vanilla to milk; stir well. Pour into 2 custard cups and sprinkle with nutmeg. Place in a pan; add water to come half way up sides of cups. Bake in 350° oven for 25 minutes or until knife inserted in custard comes out clean.

Variations: Substitute maple flavoring or almond extract for vanilla. Or, put 1 tablespoon mashed apricot or other fruit in each custard cup before pouring in custard mixture.

BANANA CUSTARD
MAKES 4 SERVINGS.

 2   cups skim milk
 1   tablespoon unflavored gelatin
 1   egg, beaten
 ½   teaspoon salt
 1   teaspoon vanilla extract
 ½   cup mashed banana
     Artificial sweetener to taste
 1   tablespoon orange juice

Heat 1½ cups of the milk in top of double boiler over hot water. Pour ½ cup cold milk in bowl and sprinkle gelatin over top. Allow to soften. Add to hot milk in top of double boiler and stir until dissolved. Add egg and cook, stirring constantly, over hot water until mixture begins to thicken (about 3 minutes). Remove from heat. Add mashed banana, orange juice, sweetener, salt, and vanilla. Chill until ready to serve.

FRESH PEACH JUBILEE
MAKES 4 SERVINGS.

 1   envelope (4-serving size) orange-flavor low-calorie gelatin
 ½   cup boiling water
 5   ice cubes
 4   unsweetened canned or fresh peach halves
 4   sprigs mint

Dissolve gelatin in ½ cup boiling water. Add ice cubes; stir until thickened, about 5 minutes. Take out unmelted ice. Beat gelatin for about 4 minutes, until thick and fluffy. Fill 4 parfait glasses half full of gelatin. Slice peach halves thinly. Arrange 1 sliced half on top of gelatin in each glass. Spoon rest of gelatin on top. Top with mint sprig. Serve chilled.

FRUIT PIE
MAKES 3 SERVINGS.

    1   envelope unflavored gelatin
    1   cup diet fruit-flavored soda
    3   apples, cored, sliced; 2 apples cored, sliced, and ½ cup
            crushed pineapple; 2 apples, cored, sliced, and ¼ cup
            blueberries; or other similar fruits in combination
    1   teaspoon ground cinnamon
        Artificial sweetener to taste
    ⅓   cup powdered skim milk
    1   tablespoon fresh lemon juice

Sprinkle gelatin over soda in bowl to soften, about 5 minutes. Stir. Add fruit, cinnamon, and sweetener to soda. Pour into 9-inch pie plate. Combine powdered skim milk, lemon juice, and sweetener to taste. Crumble mixture on top of pie. Bake 1 hour in 350° oven until golden brown.

Chocolate Desserts and Cheesecakes

HOT FUDGE SAUCE
MAKES ABOUT ⅔ CUP.

    ½   cup nonfat milk
    1   tablespoon diet margarine
    4   packets low-calorie hot cocoa mix

Heat milk and margarine in small saucepan over low heat until margarine is melted. Stir in low-calorie cocoa mix. Mix until smooth. Boil gently 1 to 2 minutes, stirring constantly, until sauce is slightly thickened.

CHOCOLATE CHIFFON
MAKES 4 SERVINGS.

> 1 cup evaporated skimmed milk
> ½ cup water
> 2 packages Alba 66 Chocolate flavor
> 1 package unflavored gelatin*
> 1 tablespoon instant coffee

Heat ½ cup of the evaporated skim milk in small saucepan; chill remainder. Combine water, chocolate flavor, gelatin, and instant coffee in bowl. Add hot milk; stir. Refrigerate until thickened. Add chilled milk. Beat until smooth. Pour into 9-inch pie dish or a bowl. Refrigerate until set.

CHOCOLATE MOUSSE PIE
MAKES 8 SERVINGS.

> ¼ cup plus ⅔ cup skim milk
> 1 envelope unflavored gelatin
> 2 eggs, separated
> 3 teaspoons cocoa
>   Artificial sweetener equal to ¼ cup sugar or less
> 1½ teaspoons vanilla extract
> 1½ cups creamed lowfat cottage cheese
> 2 tablespoons sugar
> ⅓ cup graham cracker crumbs
> ¼ teaspoon ground cinnamon
> 1 cup sliced fresh fruit

Pour the ¼ cup milk into blender. Add gelatin and allow to soften for a few minutes. Scald the ⅔ cup milk in small saucepan. Pour hot milk into blender and process just enough to combine ingredients. Allow mixture to rest for 5 minutes so gelatin can dissolve completely. Add egg yolks, cocoa, sweetener, and vanilla; process at medium speed until well-blended. Add cottage cheese and blend until smooth. Pour into bowl, cover and chill until mixture mounds from a spoon. Beat egg whites until frothy. Gradually beat in the 2 tablespoons sugar until stiff peaks form. Fold egg whites into chocolate mixture. Combine graham cracker crumbs

---

*For a thicker chiffon, use 1½ packages gelatin.

with cinnamon and sprinkle on bottom of a greased, 8-inch pie pan. Press crumbs into bottom of pan with fingers. Spoon chocolate mixture into pie shell. Chill several hours, until firm. Before serving, arrange fruit on top with additional graham cracker crumbs if desired.

CHEESECAKE #1
MAKES 6-8 SERVINGS.

    12 ounces part-skim ricotta or whey cheese or 12 ounces
            lowfat cottage cheese
    1   egg
    1   teaspoon artificial sweetener
    1   teaspoon vanilla extract
    1   teaspoon fresh lemon juice
    1   8-ounce can fruit cocktail
    1   envelope unflavored gelatin
    ¼   cup cold water

Blend cheese, egg, sweetener, vanilla, and lemon juice until creamy in blender. Add drained fruit cocktail. Sprinkle gelatin over ¼ cup cold water and let soften about 5 minutes. Combine with cheese mixture. Fill 9-inch spring pan coated with vegetable cooking spray with mixture. Bake 30 minutes in 375° oven until set. Cool and refrigerate.

CHEESECAKE #2
MAKES 4 SERVINGS.

    2   eggs
    2   cups lowfat cottage cheese
    2   teaspoons vanilla extract
    1   teaspoon lemon extract
    2   tablespoons fresh lemon juice
    2   tablespoons nonfat milk
        Artificial sweetener to equal 1 tablespoon sugar
    2   egg whites
    2   tablespoons dry skim milk
    ¼   teaspoon cream of tartar

Mix together whole eggs, cottage cheese, vanilla, lemon extract and juice, powder nonfat milk, and sweetener in large bowl. Beat egg whites, skim milk and cream of tartar until stiff peaks form.

Fold beaten whites into cheese mixture. Pour into spring-form pan. Bake at 350° for 30 to 35 minutes. Cool. Refrigerate overnight.

STRAWBERRY CHEESECAKE
SERVES 4.

- 1 teaspoon unflavored gelatin
- 1 tablespoon hot water
  Artificial sweetener to taste
- 1 cup strawberries
- 2/3 cup lowfat cottage cheese
- 1 egg white
- 1 teaspoon almond extract

Dissolve gelatin in water; add sweetener. Blend strawberries and cottage cheese in blender. Combine with gelatin mixture. Beat egg white until stiff. Add almond extract to berry mixture. Fold in egg white. Chill until set.

More Gelatin Desserts

Jello is not the Lite Way
    1 cup
    200 calories

The Lite Way
    1 tablespoon unflavored gelatin
    30 calories

Make your own "jello"
MAKES 4 SERVINGS.

- 16 ounces any flavor low-calorie or diet soda
- 1 package unflavored gelatin

Pour all but 1/4 cup soda into saucepan and heat to boiling. Combine 1/4 cup cold soda and gelatin in bowl; allow to soften. Add hot soda and stir to dissolve. Pour into dishes. Cool until jelled.

KOOL-AID JELL
MAKES 6 SERVINGS.

>3 cups water
>2 envelopes unflavored gelatin
>1 packet unsweetened Kool-Aid, any flavor
>Artificial sweetener to taste

Heat 1½ cups water in saucepan. Transfer to bowl. Dissolve gelatin, Kool-Aid, and sweetener in hot water. Add 1½ cups cold water to gelatin mixture and let cool until jelled.

COFFEE WHIP
MAKES 4 SERVINGS.

>1 envelope unflavored gelatin
>½ cup cold water (skim milk may be substituted)
>1½ cups strong black coffee, hot
>½ teaspoon vanilla extract
>Artificial sweetener to taste
>Dash salt

Sprinkle gelatin over cold water in bowl to soften, about 5 minutes. Add in hot coffee and dissolve gelatin. Add vanilla, sweetener, and salt; chill until syrupy. Beat thickened gelatin with rotary beater until it almost doubles in volume; spoon into sherbet glasses. Chill until firm.

SNOW PUDDING
MAKES 6 SERVINGS.

>1 tablespoon unflavored gelatin
>1¼ cups water
>Artificial sweetener to taste
>¼ cup fresh lemon juice
>¼ teaspoon salt
>3 egg whites

Sprinkle gelatin in ¼ cup of the cold water to soften, about 5 minutes. Heat remaining 1 cup water to boiling in saucepan. Transfer to bowl. Dissolve gelatin mixture in hot water. Dissolve sweetener in lemon juice and add to gelatin. Chill until nearly set, about ½ to ¾ hour. Add salt to egg whites, and whip until stiff. Beat gelatin mixture into egg whites, continuing to beat until it begins to thicken. Pour into bowl or individual dishes. Chill thoroughly for ½ to ¾ hour.

TOPPINGS

It's the topping on the cake that may finally be the 90 calories too much!

	Calories
1 tablespoon pecans in syrup	87
1 tablespoon butterscotch syrup	63
1 tablespoon walnuts in syrup	77
1 tablespoon fudge sauce	52
1 tablespoon whipped cream	50
1 tablespoon non-dairy whip	7–16
1 tablespoon Lite Way whipped "cream"	under 10

LITE WAY WHIPPED "CREAM"
MAKES ABOUT 4 CUPS.

- 1 teaspoon unflavored gelatin
- 2 tablespoons water
- ½ cup nonfat dry milk
- 1 cup iced water
- 1 teaspoon honey
- 1 teaspoon vanilla extract

Sprinkle gelatin over 2 tablespoons water in small saucepan to soften for about 5 minutes. Then stir over low heat to dissolve gelatin. Cool. Mix dry milk, iced water, honey, and vanilla in large bowl until smooth. Whip in gelatin mixture until light and fluffy and resembles whipped cream.

WHIPPED TOPPING #1
MAKES ABOUT 2½ CUPS TOPPING.

- ½ cup water
- 1 tablespoon fresh lemon juice
- ½ cup nonfat dry milk
- ¼ teaspoon vanilla extract
    Artificial sweetener to taste

Combine water, lemon juice, and powdered milk in bowl. Beat with electric beater until stiff. Beat in vanilla and sweetener. Chill. Use as you would whipped cream.

WHIPPED TOPPING #2

- ½ cup evaporated skim milk
- 1 teaspoon almond or vanilla extract
    Artificial sweetener to taste

Whip evaporated skim milk to consistency of whipped cream. Add almond or vanilla extract and artificial sweetener to taste.

WHIPPED TOPPING #3
MAKES ¾ CUP.

- 1½ teaspoons unflavored gelatin
- ¼ cup water
- ¼ teaspoon vanilla extract
    Artificial sweetener to taste
- ¼ cup chilled evaporated skimmed milk

Sprinkle gelatin over water in small saucepan to soften, about 5 minutes. Heat slowly, stirring, until gelatin dissolves. Pour into small mixing bowl. Add vanilla and sweetener. Cool. Add chilled milk. Beat at high speed until thick. Refrigerate.

LIME FRUIT DRESSING

MAKES ⅔ CUP.

- ½ cup low fat cottage cheese
- 2 tablespoons skim milk
- 2 teaspoons fresh lime juice
- ¼ teaspoon grated lime zest
  Artificial sweetener to taste

Blend all the ingredients together in blender. Chill.

BEVERAGES

Good health dictates a minimum of 6 to 8 glasses of liquid a day. Although water may taste good after a hot game of tennis, at other times we look for tastier drinks. And those drinks can make or break the new Lite Way of eating you have learned. Calories in common drinks range from:

		Calories per 1 cup
Herb tea	with	0
	to	
Thick shake	with	314
	and in between	
Tomato juice	with	50
Skim milk	with	88
Orange juice	with	112
A can of soda	with	150
Whole milk	with	160
Chocolate milk	with	208

Even alcoholic beverages run the calorie gamut. You can judge calories in distilled spirits—gin, rum, vodka or whiskey—by the proof marked on the label:

Proof	Calories per ounce
80	100
90	110
100	125

Wine has fewer calories. Many physicians appear to feel that a glass of wine with dinner is not only all right for dieters, but actually may be good for them. The choice of which wine to drink is obvious from the following chart:

155

Wine	Calories per 4 ounce glass
Red Bordeaux	83
White Chablis	84
Cream Sherry	164
Sweet Vermouth	176
White Port	185

GENERAL SUGGESTIONS FOR BEVERAGES

1. Drink skim milk, or 1 or 2% butterfat milk rather than whole milk.

2. Try a glass of buttermilk with lunch.

3. Cut down on calories in fruit drinks by adding seltzer or soda water.

4. Iced herb teas make a refreshing drink.

5. Fruit and melon puréed in a blender with ice make thick low-calorie shakes.

6. Try bottled sparkling water with a slice of lemon or lime.

7. Iced bouillon is a tasty drink.

8. For a hot drink try low calorie hot chocolate, which is about 50 calories a cup.

9. Half black coffee and half cocoa makes a robust hot drink. It is good iced, too.

10. A spritzer—a few ounces of wine in a glass of iced soda water—makes a glass of wine go further with fewer calories.

11. Lite beer is available commercially, but it is still 100 calories a bottle.

12. Lite wine is also now available, with about 50 calories a glass.

Whether you use it for drinking or cooking, the milk you use will vary greatly in fat and calories depending upon your choice:

1 Cup	Calories
chocolate milk	208
chocolate skim	179
regular milk	160
2 percent fat	121
1 percent fat	102
skim buttermilk	90

Many times when you think you want to snack, what you really want is a little quiet time with a cup of herb tea; it has zero calories. And there is a wide variety to choose from: rose hips, hibiscus, peppermint, chamomile, lemon, ginseng, orange, and apple among them.

ORANGE SHAKE
MAKES 2 SERVINGS.

- ½ cup crushed ice
- ½ cup orange juice
- ⅔ cup plain lowfat yogurt

Purée all the ingredients in a blender and serve at once.

APPLE FROSTIE
MAKES 1 SERVING.

- ⅔ cup cold apple juice
- ¼ cup cold skim milk
- 2 tablespoons celery juice
- 2 tablespoons fresh lemon juice

Blend all the ingredients in a blender until smooth.

PINEAPPLE SHAKE
MAKES 1 SERVING.

- 2 slices pineapple
- ½ cup skim milk
- 1 sprig fresh mint

Blend the pineapple and milk in a blender. Add mint.

ORANGE-LEMON CREAM
MAKES 1 SERVING.

- 1/2   peeled, seeded orange
- 1/2   peeled, seeded lemon
- 1/2   cup skim milk
- 2   ice cubes
    Artificial sweetener to taste

Blend all ingredients together in blender until mixture is smooth.

PEACH SHAKE
MAKES 1 SERVING.

- 1/3   cup instant nonfat dry milk
- 1/4   cup canned sliced peaches, no sugar added
- 2   tablespoons ice water
- 3   ice cubes
    Dash ground ginger

Process all the ingredients in a blender until smooth. Scrape mixture down from sides of blender container and process 1 to 2 seconds longer.

STRAWBERRY SHAKE
MAKES 1 SERVING.

- 1   cup fresh or frozen whole strawberries, no sugar added
- 6   ice cubes
- 1/2   cup ice water
- 1/3   cup instant nonfat dry milk
- 1/4   teaspoon almond extract

Process all the ingredients in a blender until smooth. Scrape mixture down from sides of container and process 1 to 2 seconds longer.

FROZEN RASPBERRY YOGURT
MAKES 4 SERVINGS.

    1   envelope unflavored gelatin
    1   cup water
    1   cup frozen raspberries, no sugar added
    1   cup plain lowfat yogurt
    $2/3$ cup instant nonfat dry milk
        Artificial sweetener equal to 3 teaspoons sugar
    $1/4$ teaspoon vanilla extract

Sprinkle gelatin over water in a small saucepan, and allow to soften, about 5 minutes. Stir over low heat, until gelatin is dissolved. Pour gelatin mixture into blender and process on low speed 2 minutes. Add remaining ingredients; process until smooth. Scrape mixture down from sides of blender and process 1 to 2 seconds longer. Pour mixture into an 8-inch square metal pan. Cover and freeze until firm, but not solid, about 1 hour. Remove from freezer. Place the mixture in the large bowl of an electric mixer or food processor; beat until smooth. Return mixture to pan; cover and freeze until firm. Scoop into serving dishes. Serve at once.

STRAWBERRY-PEAR SHAKE
MAKES 2 SERVINGS.

    1   cup fresh or unsweetened frozen strawberries
    1   ripe pear, peeled, cored, cut into chunks
    $1/2$ cup plain lowfat yogurt
    $1/2$ cup skim milk
        Artificial sweetener to equal 1 teaspoon sugar

Put all ingredients into a blender; cover and blend 40 to 50 seconds at medium speed, until smooth and frothy.

ICED COFFEE VARIATIONS
MAKES 1 SERVING.

    1   rounded teaspoon instant coffee
    $1/4$ cup boiling water

Dissolve the coffee in the water

Add:

  ³/₄ cup skim milk and dash of one of the following: vanilla, orange peel, allspice, cinnamon.
   OR
  ³/₄ cup water and dash of one of the following: rum flavoring, skim milk, cinnamon.

PINEAPPLE FLIP
SERVES 1.

  ¼ cup cold orange juice
  ¼ cup cold pineapple juice
  ¼ cup cold skim milk

Combine ingredients in blender or small bowl. Beat till frothy.

GREAT GRAPE
SERVES 1.

  ½ cup skim milk
  ¼ cup unsweetened grape juice
  1 teaspoon fresh lemon juice
     Artificial sweetener to taste

Blend until smooth.

CRANBERRY SURPRISE
SERVES 1.

  ½ cup unsweetened cranberry juice
  ⅓ cup skim milk
  1 egg white
     Artificial sweetener to taste

Blend in blender until smooth.

HOT CHOCOLATE
SERVES 2.

>   1   tablespoon cocoa
>   1   tablespoon instant coffee
>   Dash salt
>   ½   teaspoon vanilla extract
>   ½   cup water
>   Artificial sweetener to taste
>   2   cups skim milk
>   Cinnamon stick

Heat first six ingredients to boiling in saucepan. Add skim milk and cinnamon stick and heat through.

BETWEEN-MEAL SNACKS

Breakfast may be the most important meal of the day; lunch, the most hurried; and dinner, the time for families, or a more leisurely meal. But between meal snacks have become the most popular. Candy bars, cookies, salty nibbles, fast foods, and recently health foods have developed billion dollar industries that cater to America's habit of snacking. For some people they replace regular meals; for others they are a way of life. Junk-food snacks have become so all consuming—and all consumed—that many schools have banned the dispensers that spew them out.

While the nibbles on which we snack are generally high sugar or high starch foods, it is all but impossible to cut them out altogether. We generally need something between meals—for a quick pick-me-up, for relaxation, for a few shared minutes among friends. But coffee and Danish? Cookies and hot cocoa? A handful of peanuts or a candy bar? No.

Is there anything left? Yes. The Lite Way can provide snacks that bring joy back into your eating, with a minimum of calories and a maximum of taste.

•Not a doughnut . . . . .200 calories
•Not a bag of potato chips . . . . .300 calories
•Not a can of soda .150 calories
                                                (average)
•Not a chocolate bar . . . . .400 calories

GENERAL SUGGESTIONS FOR SNACKS

1. Use fresh fruit for snacking whenever possible.
2. Avoid granola with added sugar.
3. Make pop corn—it is filled with fiber and air, not calories. But hold the butter and watch out for the salt.
4. Try a little peanut butter spread on apple slices.
5. Nibble a piece of reduced calorie gruyère cheese with a pear.
6. Spread a low calorie cracker with cottage cheese and a touch of jelly.
7. Drink herb tea in all its wonderful flavors.
8. Eat a celery stalk stuffed with cottage cheese or limited amount of peanut butter.
9. Dip raw carrots and cucumber slices into yogurt dip.
10. Eat a few pretzels—they are no more caloric than a diet cracker.
11. Limit the portion of your snack before you begin to eat. Store 1½-ounce portions of your favorite snacks in small plastic bags, instead of reaching for: 1 cup of nuts (700 to 1000 calories), 1 cup of pumpkin sunflower seeds (700 to 800 calories), 1 cup dried fruit (400 to 600 calories).

12. Nibbler's Bowl:
    green pepper
    celery
    radishes
    cucumber
    cauliflower
    string beans
    cherry tomato
    carrots
    turnip

Cut vegetables and any fruit into bite-size pieces. Combine in bowl. Nibble away.

Nibble and Snack the Lite Way

CRACKER SNACKS

Place bits of Sapsago cheese on Armenian crackerbread (Lovash). Broil until bubbly.

BREAD CUPS

Cut very thin bread into 3-inch circles and place into small muffin tins. Bake in 375° oven 10 minutes. Sprinkle with grated Sapsago. Fill with chopped cooked spinach, or chopped tomato or vegetable of your choice. Sprinkle with herbs and imitation bacon bits. Heat in 400° oven until thoroughly heated, about 20 minutes.

FROZEN FRUIT OR JUICE

One-half small banana on a popsicle stick dipped in fruit juice, rolled in wheat germ, and frozen.

Crush frozen fruit in blender and serve in paper cup as a fruit slush.

Pour fruit juice into ice cube trays with inserts. Freeze 10 minutes; stick toothpicks into compartments and freeze as popsicle.

NIBBLES

½   cup plain lowfat yogurt and
1   teaspoon artificial sweetener or 1 teaspoon honey or a few drops of one of the following:
    Rum extract
    Vanilla extract
    Chocolate extract
    Maple extract

(GARP)

1   pack straight pretzels
2   cups shredded wheat bits
2   cups Cheerios
2   cups pop corn
1   tablespoon Worcestershire sauce
    Onion salt to taste
1   tablespoon imitation bacon bits

Spread pretzels, wheat bits, cheerios, and pop corn on cookie sheet. Sprinkle on Worcestershire sauce, onion salt. Bake in 300° oven 1 hour. Last half hour add 1 tablespoon imitation bacon bits.

GOING THE LITE WAY

- Sprinkle small potato skins with grated Parmesan cheese. Add chives, garlic powder, scallions, or imitation bacon bits as preferred. Broil.
- Frozen blueberries, banana or grapes.
- For homemade diet lemonade, squeeze fresh lemon juice, and add low-cal sweetener and sparkling water.
- Tangy bite-sized cubes of tomato aspic. Follow directions on an unflavored gelatin package, adding 1 to 2 cups tomato juice seasoned with Worcestershire sauce.
- Brown yogurt on bagel chips with minced chives (or favorite herb) and sprinkle of grated Parmesan cheese.
- Sip bouillon, chicken broth, or try jellied "madrilene."
- Try using butter flavoring or garlic on popcorn.
- Boil up an artichoke—it takes ages to eat. Dip in fresh lemon juice spiced with garlic.
- Nibble ½ cup blueberries or strawberries, ¼ cantaloupe or honeydew, or 1 cup of watermelon chunks.

Low Calorie Combinations (100 calories or less.)

- ¼ cup low fat cottage cheese plus ¼ cup chopped pears, peaches, unsweetened pineapple
- 1 ounce melted skim milk mozzarella plus 3 unsalted Saltines
- 1 ounce reduced calorie American cheese plus ½ small apple or 12 unsalted pretzel sticks
- ⅔ cup plain lowfat yogurt plus ½ cup mandarin orange sections
- 1 cup skim milk plus 1 graham cracker
- 1 frozen lowfat yogurt pop (60 to 70 calories) plus ¾ cup unbuttered popcorn
- 12 ounces Alba "77" shake plus 3 unsalted ring pretzels
- 1 cup Alba "66" hot cocoa plus 10 oyster crackers or 1 graham cracker

- ½ level tablespoon peanut butter plus ½ small apple or 1 slice thin whole grain bread or 2 rye thin crackers*
- ⅔ cup plain lowfat yogurt plus ¼ cup unsweetened pineapple
- ⅔ cup plain lowfat yogurt plus ½ small apple with cinnamon or ½ cup strawberries
- ½ level tablespoon peanut butter plus ½ slice raisin bread
- ½ level tablespoon peanut butter plus 2 Wheat Thins plus ½ cup skim milk
- 1 ounce reduced calorie Gruyère cheese plus ½ small pear
- ¼ cup lowfat cottage cheese plus ½ cup blueberries
- 1 ounce reduced calorie cheese melted on 1 slice very thin whole-grain bread
- ¼ cup lowfat cottage cheese plus 1 sliced apricot
- 1 ounce diced lowfat mozzarella cheese plus 10 oyster crackers
- 1 fruit frappe (blend ½ cup fresh strawberries and 1 cup skim milk in the blender)
- California flip (blend ¼ cup orange juice and ¼ cup skim milk in blender)
- ¼ cup lowfat cottage cheese plus ½ slice thin raisin bread
- Blend 1-inch banana slice plus ½ cup skim milk plus 1 teaspoon peanut butter in blender
- ¼ cup lowfat cottage cheese plus 1-inch banana slice mashed
- ½ cup skim milk plus 2 teaspoons peanut butter on 1 crisp whole grain cracker (Thin Crisp)*
- one of the fruit, milk, or fruit-milk combination desserts in the dessert chapter

*There are many new Lite Way crackers available under 20 calories each. Look for whole grain crisp varieties to add to your Lite Way snack alternatives.

Dips

For parties, have vegetable "nibblers" such as cauliflower flower-ets, cherry tomatoes, raw string beans, carrot and celery sticks, cucumber slices and sticks, scallions, mushroom caps, zucchini sticks, radish roses, and red and green pepper strips.

PIMENTO DIP
MAKES 1½ CUPS.

- 1 cup pimentos
- 2 tablespoons cider vinegar
- 2 tablespoons prepared mustard
  Artificial sweetener to equal 4 teaspoons sugar

Combine all ingredients in blender; process until smooth. Chill.

YOGURT-CUCUMBER DIP
MAKES 2 CUPS.

- 1 cup plain lowfat yogurt
- ½ cup shredded iceburg lettuce
- ¼ cup finely chopped, pared, seeded cucumber
- 1 large clove garlic, minced
- 1 teaspoon salt
- 1 teaspoon chopped fresh mint leaves or ½ teaspoon dried
- ¼ teaspoon white pepper

In small bowl, combine yogurt, lettuce, and cucumber. Combine garlic and salt in small bowl to make a paste; stir in 2 tablespoons yogurt mixture. Add to remaining yogurt mixture; mix well. Season with mint and pepper.

ONION DIP
MAKES 2 CUPS.

> 1 cup plain lowfat yogurt
> 1 cup lowfat cottage cheese
> 3 tablespoons dry onion soup mix
> 1/4 teaspoon chili powder

In medium bowl, combine yogurt and cottage cheese until well blended. Stir in soup mix and chili powder. Refrigerate dip, covered, 3 hours. Arrange on tray with crisp vegetables or chilled shrimp.

MEDITERRANEAN DIP
MAKES 1/2 CUP.

> 1/4 teaspoon Italian Seasoning (page 24)
> 1/4 teaspoon minced onion
> 1/4 teaspoon snipped chives
> 1 tablespoon hot water
> 1/3 cup lowfat cottage cheese

Combine seasoning, onion, chives, and hot water in blender. Let stand 1 minute. Add cottage cheese. Process at medium speed for 2 minutes or until ingredients are well blended. Chill in small dish.

SPECIAL OCCASION COTTAGE CHEESE DIP
MAKES 1/2 CUP.

> 12 ounces lowfat cottage cheese
> Skim or butter milk
> Chopped scallions
> Snipped chives and/or onion

Blend cottage cheese in blender. Add enough skim milk or butter-milk to give mixture spreading consistency. Add finely chopped scallions, chives and/or onion. Chill. Serve with raw vegetables.

RAW VEGETABLE DIP
MAKES ½ CUP.

         2 green onions, chopped
        ¼ cup sliced red pepper
         4 sprigs fresh parsley
         1 teaspoon dill weed
            Dash salt
        ½ cup part-skim ricotta cheese

Process all ingredients except cheese in blender at high speed until finely chopped, about 10 to 15 seconds. Add cheese and process until well mixed, about 15 seconds longer. Serve with raw vegetables.

YOGURT DIP VARIATION
MAKES 1¼ CUPS.

         1 cup plain lowfat yogurt
         1 tablespoon horseradish
         2 tablespoons Dijon-style mustard
         1 teaspoon Italian Seasoning (page 24)

Blend and chill.

VARIETY DIPS

         2 cups lowfat cottage cheese
        ½ cup buttermilk or plain lowfat yogurt or Lite Way Farmer
               Whipped Cream Cheese (page 172)
            Pinch salt
         1 teaspoon fresh lemon juice

Blend all ingredients in blender until smooth. Add any of the following:
         canned minced clams, drained and seasoned with
         ½ teaspoon Tabasco
         chives
         bleu cheese or roquefort
         parsley
         vegetable soup mix (Knorr)
         onion soup mix

Season with herbs to taste:
- curry powder
- garlic powder
- horseradish
- grated onion or onion flakes
- dry mustard or prepared mustard
- garlic or garlic powder
- dill
- scallions

"LOOK ALIKES"

Do you want to have some fun? Try the Look Alike game—make fattening old favorites that aren't fattening at all, but are still delicious.

LITE WAY LOOK ALIKES

	Calories
Sour Cream, regular 1 ounce	50–60
non butterfat	35–40
Lite Way	Under 30
Mayonnaise, regular 1 tablespoon	95–100
imitation	40
Lite Way	Under 30
Whipped Cream, regular 2 tablespoons	58
whipped topping	7–16
Lite Way	Under 10
Cream Cheese, regular	100–110
imitation	50–60
whipped	70–80
Lite Way	Under 50

CHEESE CRUNCHIES
MAKES 1 SERVING.

    1   ounce reduced calorie hard cheese

Dice cheese into small cubes, and place about 1 inch apart on non-stick cookie sheet. Bake in 350° oven for 5 minutes. Cool 6 to 8 minutes until cheese holds it shape. Serve warm.

LITE WAY FARMER WHIPPED CREAM CHEESE

Process 8-ounce package of farmer cheese (or dry, uncreamed pot cheese or cottage cheese) in a blender or food processor, for 2 to 3 minutes, until every bit of graininess disappears and the cheese has the consistency of a whipped cream or fluffy frosting. (Some farmer cheese is salt-free; for a flavor more like conventional cream cheese, add a pinch of salt or butter flavoring.) Scoop whipped cheese into container; cover and store in refrigerator. The whipped cheese stiffens as it chills.

"MAPLE SYRUP"
MAKES ¾ CUP.

    1   tablespoon cornstarch
    2   tablespoons cold water
    1   cup boiling water
    1   teaspoon maple flavoring
    2   teaspoons liquid sweetener
        Dash salt

Blend cornstarch and 2 tablespoons cold water in saucepan. Add 1 cup boiling water and maple flavoring. Boil 5 minutes until syrupy. Add sweetener and salt.

LITE WAY SOUR CREAM #1
MAKES ⅓ CUP.

    ⅓   cup lowfat cottage cheese
    2   tablespoons water
    ½   teaspoon fresh lemon juice
        Dash salt

Blend all the ingredients in blender until smooth.

LITE WAY SOUR CREAM #2
MAKES ABOUT 1½ CUPS.

    1   container (8 ounces) pot cheese
    ¾   cup buttermilk
        Dash salt

Process ingredients in blender at high speed until smooth and creamy. Once during blending, stop blender and scrape down sides of container with rubber spatula. Refrigerate. Mixture will keep several days.

LITE WAY SOUR CREAM #3
MAKES 2½ CUPS.

    1½ cups 1% fat cottage cheese
    1   tablespoon fresh lemon juice
    ½   cup water
    ½   cup buttermilk, or plain lowfat yogurt

Process all ingredients in blender until smooth.

EGG FOO YOUNG
MAKES 4 SERVINGS.

    1   cup beansprouts
    ½   cup chopped scallion
    ½   cup chopped green pepper
    ¼   cup sliced water chestnuts
        Leftover chicken, shrimp, etc.
    4   eggs, beaten
    1   tablespoon soy sauce

Combine all the ingredients in a bowl. Heat in nonstick pan coated with vegetable cooking spray over medium heat. Drop in mixture by tablespoonfuls and cook on both sides until brown.

BAKED "FRIED" FISH
MAKES 4 SERVINGS.

- ½   cup skim milk
- 1   teaspoon salt
- ½   teaspoon Worcestershire sauce
- 2   teaspoons minced onion
- ½   cup dry bread crumbs
- ½   teaspoon paprika
- ¼   teaspoon dry mustard
- 1½   pounds sole fillets

MIx milk, salt, Worcestershire, and onion in bowl. Combine bread crumbs, paprika and mustard on piece of waxed paper. Dip fish in milk mixture, then in crumb mixture, coating both sides. Place in baking nonstick pan. Bake in 400° oven for 20 minutes until golden brown.

SWEET "ROLL"
MAKES 2 SERVINGS.

- 2   eggs, separated
- ½   cup evaporated skimmed milk
-   Artificial sweetener to taste
- ¼   teaspoon ground cinnamon
- ¼   teaspoon orange peel, grated
- ⅛   teaspoon ground nutmeg
- ¼   teaspoon vanilla extract

Beat egg whites until stiff peaks are formed. Set aside. Combine egg yolks and remaining ingredients in blender and blend until smooth. Fold into egg whites and blend. Pour into nonstick muffin pans. Bake in 350° oven for about 20 minutes or until firm.

SOUTHERN "FRIED" CHICKEN
MAKES 4 SERVINGS.

- 4   slices toast
- 1   teaspoon parsley, chopped fresh
- ½   teaspoon poultry seasoning

> 4 skinned boneless chicken breasts (8 ounces each)
> 1 teaspoon salt
> Dash pepper
> ½ cup skim milk

Roll toast into crumbs with rolling pin. Combine with parsley and seasoning. Sprinkle chicken with salt and pepper. Pour milk into bowl. Immerse each piece of chicken in milk, then roll in crumb mixture, making sure chicken is coated. Place on nonstick baking pan. Distribute remaining milk or crumbs over chicken. Bake in 375° oven for 30 minutes until golden brown.

"BANANA SPLIT"
MAKES 1 SERVING.

> 8⅔ tablespoons nonfat dry milk (⅔ cup minus 2 tablespoons)
> 10 tablespoons ice water
> Artificial sweetener to taste
> 2 teaspoons banana extract
> food coloring
> ½ small banana, sliced
> Crushed pineapple sauce (recipe follows)
> Sweetened Strawberries (recipe follows)
> Whipped Topping (page 153)

Place dry milk in deep bowl or 1 quart measuring cup. Add ice water, sweetener, and extract. Beat at low speed for 1 minute, then high speed until mixture is consistency of thick cream. Chill in freezer for 3 hours or until firm and similar to ice cream. In a parfait glass alternate layers of banana mixture with sliced bananas, pineapple sauce, and strawberries. Top with whipped topping.

CRUSHED PINEAPPLE SAUCE
MAKES 1 SERVING.

> ¼ fresh medium pineapple, finely shredded
> 2 tablespoons water

Combine pineapple and water. Chill.

SWEETENED STRAWBERRIES
MAKES 1 SERVING.

> ½   cup strawberries
>   Artificial sweetener to taste

Reserve 3 strawberries for garnish. Combine remaining strawberries with sweetener.

"POTATO PANCAKES"
SERVES 2.

> 1   package (10 ounces) frozen cauliflower
> ½   cup lowfat cottage cheese
> 1   slice white bread
> 2   tablespoons minced fresh onion
> ½   teaspoon salt
>   Dash pepper

Cook cauliflower according to package directions. Drain. Blend with cottage cheese, bread, onion, and salt and pepper in blender until smooth. Spoon 6 patties onto nonstick cookie sheet. Bake in 350° oven for 25 minutes, until brown and crisp. Serve with Applesauce Topping.

APPLESAUCE TOPPING FOR PANCAKES

> 1   medium apple
> 3   tablespoons water
> ½   teaspoon fresh lemon juice
>   Dash ground cinnamon
>   Artificial sweetener to taste

Core and chop apple. Blend apple, water, lemon juice and cinnamon in blender until smooth. Add sweetener. Boil in pan for 2 minutes. Stir; cool.

LASAGNA WITHOUT NOODLES
MAKES 2 SERVINGS.

1¼	pounds ground beef
	Salt
	Pepper
2	cups lowfat cottage cheese
2	eggs
2	cups shredded part-skim mozzarella cheese
2	cups marinara sauce (page 126)

Brown beef in nonstick skillet. Add salt and pepper. Drain fat. Mix cottage cheese with eggs in small bowl. In a 2½ quart baking dish, layer meat with cottage cheese mixture, marinara, and mozzarella. Bake in 350° oven for 45 minutes.

FRENCH "FRIES"

1	can (8 ounces) Italian green beans, well drained
½	teaspoon salt

Place beans on cookie sheet; make sure they do not overlap. Sprinkle with ¼ teaspoon salt. Bake in 400° oven for 10 minutes or until beans are brown and crisp. Remove from oven. Sprinkle with remaining salt.

MOCK SPLIT PEA SOUP
MAKES 4 SERVINGS.

1	can (8 ounces) asparagus
1	can (8 ounces) string beans
	Liquid from one of cans
	Salt and pepper to taste
	Oregano to taste

Blend all the ingredients in blender. Transfer to saucepan and heat.

LITE WAY MAYONNAISE #1

1   cup lowfat cottage cheese
2   tablespoons fresh lemon juice
2   egg yolks
1/2   teaspoon Italian Seasoning (page 24)
1/2   teaspoon salt
    Cayenne pepper
1/2   teaspoon dry mustard
1/4   teaspoon onion powder or 1/2 teaspoon grated onion

Blend all ingredients together in blender. Chill.

LITE WAY MAYONNAISE #2
MAKES 1 1/4 CUPS.

1/2   teaspoon unflavored gelatin
1   chicken bouillon cube
1/4   cup boiling water
1   cup buttermilk

Dissolve gelatin and bouillon cube in boiling water in small bowl. Let cool a few minutes. Stir in buttermilk. Chill in refrigerator until mixture is slightly firm.

LITE WAY TARTAR SAUCE
MAKES 1 SERVING.

Combine 1 tablespoon Lite Way Mayonnaise #1 with minced washed capers, chopped fresh parsley, dry mustard, and snipped fresh chives. Thin with fresh lemon juice or thicken with measured amount of tomato paste or minced vegetables such as cucumber, green pepper, or spinach. Good over fish.

DRAWN "BUTTER"

MAKES ¼ CUP.

- 1 teaspoon unflavored gelatin
- ⅛ cup cold water
- ⅛ cup hot water
- ¼ teaspoon imitation butter flavoring
- 1 teaspoon nonfat dry milk
- ¼ teaspoon salt
- 2 drops yellow food coloring

Sprinkle gelatin over cold water in small saucepan to soften, about 5 minutes. Add hot water. Cook over low heat until gelatin is dissolved. Stir in remaining ingredients. Cook 1 minute.

"GRAVY" FOR CHICKEN

MAKES 1 CUP.

- ½ cup skim milk
- ½ teaspoon imitation butter flavoring
- ½ cup chicken bouillon or Lite Way Chicken Stock (page 26)
- ½ teaspoon onion powder

Combine all ingredients in small saucepan. Cook over low heat for 5 minutes.

CHOPPED VEGETARIAN "LIVER"

MAKES 1 SERVING.

- 1 small onion, chopped, or 2 tablespoons onion flakes
- ½ pound string beans, cooked
  Bouillon
- 2 hard-boiled eggs, chopped
  Salt and pepper to taste

Cook onion in bouillon in saucepan until tender. Drain. Combine onion with string beans. Chop and add to chopped eggs. Season with salt and pepper. Chill.

Index

ABOUT THE AUTHORS

JUDITH R. CORLIN, Ed.M., R.D., is nutrition consultant for the Scarsdale Medical Group. Also a noted educator and lecturer, she is a nutritionist previously associated with the Tufts University Department of Preventive Medicine, the Harvard School of Public Health, Peter Bent Brigham Hospital, and the New England Medical Center Hospital. She participated in the White House Conference on Food and Nutrition. Ms. Corlin is currently nutrition consultant for the Health Insurance Plan of Greater New York and is in private practice in Scarsdale, New York.

MARY SUSAN MILLER is the author of five other books, including *Bringing Learning Home* and *Childstress.* She has been a regular contributor to leading magazines and currently writes for *Good Housekeeping.* She is a frequent guest on many television shows.